LETTER TO A YOUNG MEDIUM

Written by Brian E. Bowles

Foreword by Minister Colin Bates

CONTENTS

COPYRIGHT PAGE

Disclaimer: The information in this book is not a substitute for medical attention, examination, diagnosis, or treatment. None of the statements in this program are meant to replace the advice of your health care professional or medical doctor. Before doing any self-reflection program, please consult with your health care provider.

Some of the names and incidents in this book have been changed to protect the privacy of individuals and to accommodate the literary flow of the book.

First E-Book Edition January 2020
Foreword by Minister Colin Bates
ISBN: 978-1-64786-648-8 (Ebook)
Published by Through the Woods Press, Inc.
Ferndale, Washington

FOREWORD

by Minister Colin Bates

Brian has created from the well of the heart a story of life unfolding on a journey that truly never ends. Together, we experience life in all of it's facets taking us to unknown places and blessing us with untold riches.

People come into our lives be it for a reason, a season or a lifetime, however long the association. Maybe, the memories and experiences become a part of who we are. As mediums, we are the story tellers of life, bringing to life the stories of all those who have travelled this path called life before us. Each story is as varied and important as our own.

In reading Brian's story, I have been deeply touched by his honesty and his understanding the sacredness of mediumship and life's journey.

In Brian's words
"As you venture into this journey of the heart, you realize that mediumship is love having the final say."

Colin Bates

DEDICATION

I dedicate this book to the development circle that taught me about chosen family. We are always "young" in this journey, but our love has a quality of the ancients. When leaning against the spine of a redwood tree, I knew I was a tiny cell against her magical trunk.

With all of you, I am part of the ancient forest of wise ones, even as my young spirit holds closely to yours. We are something far greater together and our light creates a temple for souls to speak and express healings that have forever changed me. Our arms in one another nurturing the other has created a strength in this calling I never imagined for myself. That island was lonely, and you were there to hold me on new shores.

Thank you, Colleen, Mikey, Salma, Alyce, Nancy, Denise, and Mardi. This original circle still holds me in some dimension in some magical meadow, even as our human lives journey in different rivers and tides. Though new souls have entered our circle and some have needed to depart, I can still feel your light in the darkest of canyons.

This has made all the difference.

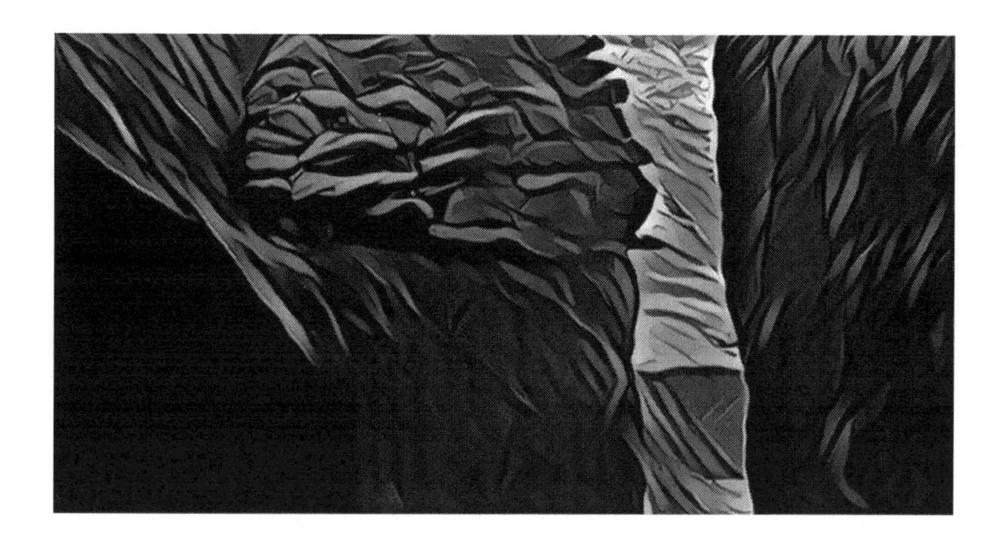

INTRODUCTION

The Night When Only High Heels Would Do

Once upon a time,

Late one October when the fall leaves held their place longer than usual due to a prolonged period of warm weather, I was hiking in Zion National Park in the stunning red rock wilderness of Utah. I decided to hike The Narrows, where two-thousand-foot cliff walls rise out of the Earth in an undulating narrow slot canyon. This is the most popular national park in the United States, and the Narrows Hike is considered one of the top ten hikes in the world, according to Outside Magazine. This was a moment to be treasured, and I came prepared. I traveled with my very fancy rental gear, including water sandal hiking shoe thingies (a hybrid of many shoes that someone far smarter than me will need to describe), a farmer john wetsuit (Picture coveralls made with black neoprene.), and a walking stick. I looked like Gay Gandalf waiting for his quest!

For $49, I had been well-prepared by a local merchant to venture into any canyon. I was doing a canyoneering course with this same local company out of Springfield, Utah, and I'd just had three days of hanging on ropes over 200 foot cliff walls and descending into canyons that left me searching for words or a paintbrush to try to respond to the beauty these ancient canyons inspired in me. My guide, Sexy Jeff Why Can't You Be Gay, told me that very day as we walked out of Birch Canyon to do a gentle walk into the Narrows. He said, "Get to know a canyon by foot first, so you respect the complexity of her walls. Remember the walls have been formed by rivers over millions of years, being carved by floods over time." Sexy Jeff Why Can't You Be Gay had never given me bad advice, and I wanted some time to myself where I didn't have to worry about wrapping up rope properly, doing perfect figure-eight knots, or practicing an ascending technique due to a poorly constructed anchor in the previous drop.

You see, Sexy Jeff Why Can't You Be Gay, was the kind of teacher who trusted nature to offer the lesson you needed. His way of teaching me was to let me make the mistakes canyoneers make, and then he would assist me in solving the problem I created. He let me descend a 120-foot wall, knowing my previous anchor would offer so much friction to the rope, that I wouldn't be able to free the rope. After we descended the 120-foot wall, he stood by and observed me pulling and pulling on the rope with no movement, not even an inch, until he said, "Do you think it should be this hard?" This was always how a new lesson launched. We'd end our days together eating an orange, and he'd say "A new journey into any canyon is always where you encounter your humanity. Mother Nature always wins, so if you forget you're her student, you will often wind up on your ass, sometimes permanently." Before we'd get in our cars at our starting point of a canyon, often after a hellaciously long hike out, he'd hug me and say, "I'm proud of you, brother." I believed him. I was finding new parts of my confidence and stability on those ropes with his gentle and wise countenance.

This day, he added with a gentle nod, "Brian, enjoy the Narrows. That canyon is a different hike every time. See you tomorrow morning at 8 AM sharp."

To avoid the huge crowds the Narrows hike attracts, I got the crazy idea to hike into this slot canyon as the afternoon sun was setting, so I could see the way the sun hits the walls of the canyon at angles that make photographers frustrated with the difference between the human eye and the human experience. It was late October, and I was the lone hiker going up the Virgin River as a few final hikers and photographers from the day were going the opposite direction. A few commented by saying, "Are you sure you should be going up the canyon at this hour?" or "Do you know when the last shuttle bus leaves from the Temple of Sinawava?" as if they were channeling my mother. I confidently smiled and left them with the impression that I knew exactly what I was doing. Couldn't they see the stellar outfit and the fancy gear?

The last shuttle bus was at 9:45 P.M. and it was the last stop on the shuttle service offered in the national park. It was 4:30 PM, so I imagined I had plenty of time. After all, the walk to the entry into the Narrows was one mile of a solid concrete path, and getting to the tributary canyon – called Orderville, was where I was planning on turning back around for my low key 3-mile roundtrip river hike. The one mile to the river and back made this entire hike only 5 miles, which was hardly a long-distance hike.

As I ventured deeper and deeper into the canyon, the sun painted dark red shadows across the sunset orange walls and I lost myself in the rippling waves of carved angles and deeper reliefs, showing the highest points of flash floods. I had made it all the way to Orderville Canyon, watching a small stream of water flow into the large river that was my trail. The enticing sanctuary of color up ahead was too enticing for me to pass up. I decided to walk further up the Wall Street section, and the darker walls and dramatic keyholes that reminded me of Georgia O'Keefe paintings left me with my mouth agape and every turn ahead seemed darker and more dramatic. Some walls turned black with arteries of blood red and violet flowing through the rocks.

I suddenly started to notice that seeing through the water to the rocks below was becoming much harder, and the remaining light seemed to almost reflect off the surface, making the inner depth almost impossible to discern. I started to notice the oranges fading to deeper reds and violets. I then realized the sun was barely hitting the tops of the canyon wall. It happened so quickly. I was likely 2 miles up the canyon and the darkness quickly descended. I was now in a racing river with 2,000-foot walls of darkness closing in on me and I was becoming more and more disoriented. *What about flash floods? Wasn't it raining north of here?*

I turned around and the canyon that I had just traveled looked completely unfamiliar. Nothing looked the same, and the dark section of Wall Street now felt like a cave of darkness. I vigorously tried to rush through the canyon. Let's just say that I am not the most graceful person I know. I don't think God gave me hips. She must have run out that day, so I am what some would describe as "Ridiculously and Insanely Clumsy". Now, add a racing river, a wetsuit, the damn sandal/shoe/water socks/heaviest shoes from hell, and let's just say I realized I had forgotten the most important tool – a headlamp. I could feel my sense of humor fading as the light on the walls now painted grey and purple shadows against a now unfamiliar canyon as images of frightened faces and elongated mouths filled the landscape of my nightmares. The surface of the water was now a dark silver stream barely reflecting any light, and the underworld of rocks and valleys was now completely invisible to me. I tried to use my walking cane to predict the depth, but it often ignored large boulders or sandy drops.

As I placed my feet one at a time into the flowing river, the depth had become impossible to gauge, and my eyes began to see only the reflection of the last remaining light bouncing off the impenetrable abyss. I stepped left and I hit a deeper section, and my walking stick was dislodged from my hand. I realized I couldn't even see where it went. I had to accept the obvious; the darkness had descended. I could see the gleaming stars above, but there was no moonlight to bounce off the 2,000 foot walls. I was wading in the darkness, and the October sky went darker far more quickly than I ever imagined. I started to envision the angle of the sun as the Earth shifts seasons, and I realized that small angle of the Earth's arc would be the margin of error that made this journey life threatening. I know! At this point, you're thinking, "Where's your flashlight, idiot?" Let's just say the Boy Scouts were not allowing gay boys at the time, so I blame them completely.

My view of the glassy dark surface of the river appeared to be running in both directions. My mind convinced me it was going both ways depending on what feature I chose to focus. I then started to question the very direction I was heading and wondered if I had started out the wrong way back. Up became down, and down became up. As I held out my right hand, I noticed that the silhouette of the perimeter of my hand was barely decipherable with my eyes, and the fear found a new staircase lower than the basement. It's that space where you are breathing but not feeling. My ears seemed to be hearing the very movement of air across my lungs as my mind began to focus.

Walk down river, Brian! Walk down river! This inner voice confronted my fear, and I trusted that I was to go down the river and go with the flow. The canyon opened up at the base, so I needed to follow the flow. I could feel the direction of the river with my hand, but I didn't trust it. I walked step by step through the river, and I felt the sandy wall going up. I fell on my knees as I realized I had found a small island of sand against one of the turns of the canyon wall. I could barely make out the specter of the tree above me. There was no shadow, because there was no light coming down into the canyon. However, the shape of the tree slowly flowed into my vision. I crawled onto the sandbar and approached the lone tree. I leaned against it for a while just to catch my breath and get my thoughts together. The crunching of the autumn leaves crackled as my butt searched for a comfortable place to land against this tree. Then, I got an idea.

I saw an image of newspaper boats we would release into the lake near City Park in Denver and watch as the winds carried them further away from the shore. I reached down and collected the leaves in my arms and shoved as many as I could into my shell jacket that was covering the wetsuit. I tightened my jacket at the bottom with a pull and filled it with leaves. As I re-entered the much colder running water of the Virgin River with the wind racing through the capillaries of this canyon in sudden bursts, I placed a leaf on the water and watched it as long as my eyes could. I would lose the leaf only 5 feet from my body, but seeing the leaf glide on the surface let me know I was going the right way. Every time I placed a leaf in the water, I felt more and more at peace. The crippling anxiety was now five feet away, but I was beginning to trust this river and feel the weight of the force gently pushing me forward. I placed a leaf, and I followed it until my frenzied mind told me that I needed another.

I briefly paused in the river and looked above. It was a new moon, which means there isn't a moon at all. Why do we call it a new moon when it offers no light? But, I saw the stars above this canyon, and they now looked like a river. The walls that careened sideways to the left and right now framed the firmament above, and I realized the darkness could get no darker. I noted to myself that the darkness of that sky allowed me to see the stars in a way I had never seen in the past, but the dark proved the distance from the stars to me was greater than I have ever comprehended. The river surface had joined the blackness and my eyes were now relying on memory and imagination, as the gentle push of the river coaxed me step by step towards an uncertain exit.

I released another leaf, and I could no longer see them travel in front of me. I just trusted they were marking the pathway ahead.

I began to hear the waterfall that was roughly a half mile from the exit point. I was elated. I knew this waterfall well. This was the stunning spot where rappelers doing the hike called Mystery Canyon would end their canyon trip by dropping on ropes through this very waterfall. I had seen multiple groups rappel down their ropes and cheered them on as they unhooked their carabiner to drop into the deepest part of this canyon. A huge flash flood from the previous year had changed the water flow in this particular section, and it was now much deeper. I needed to place my backpack on top of my head on the way through this section.

How the hell can I carry my pack and drop the leaves to guide my way?

My leaf technique wouldn't work through this narrow part, and I would need to ensure I kept my backpack above the water flow. So, I opened my jacket and began to adjust my backpack, and all of the remaining leaves I had stuffed in my jacket were now released. I immediately tried to grab them back in my arms just in case I needed them, but they were already riding the small rapids of the river. They were completely out of my sight as soon as the fear gripped me.

They likely never were in my real vision, but my imagined path had forever changed. The constant stream of the waterfall was once comforting, but now it felt like a siren that assured my doomed fate. As I tried to push out my thoughts of fear and terror, I raised my hands and began to cry. I began thrashing and screaming at the sky, knowing that this wall through this narrow section would then immediately open back into a section of the river where my direction could become confused once again. I yelled, "Fucking help me!" in my final surrender to the river.

It was in that moment that I felt his presence. Alan (AKA Miss Alexis the Drag Queen Who Outperformed any Other Madonna

Impersonator) laughed as he approached, echoing off the canyon walls as he came closer and closer. He showed me himself as Alan without the makeup, hair, and stunning nails. His dyed blonde hair and dark eyebrows from a heavy pencil He smiled and then turned around like Wonder Woman changing her outfit, and then Miss Alexis appeared in all her glory. Her long purple formal dress shimmered in a light from an unknown source, and her long flowing black hair with the perfect amount of wave and movement framed her face. She was not impersonating Madge this evening. She was full-blown Miss Alexis.

"Really, Bitch?," landed on my ears and I felt embarrassed as I began to laugh.
I replied by simply saying, "I know, right?"
Miss Alexis continued the deposition, saying, "Girl, why are you in a cold ass river at night in Utah? In Utah? You couldn't choose a night hike in Miami? They have beaches there and gay people and rainbow flags everywhere."
I pleaded, "Can you help me?"
She replied, "Honey, I am no fairy godmother, but I know I can help you."
I replied, "I'm so afraid I won't survive this. The river is about to get deeper, and I have no idea how to take one step. What if I go back up river? I can barely see my hand directly in front of my eyes!"
"You don't always need your eyes to see. Close your eyes and trust the movement of the river. Feel it guide you with every step. I will be right beside you in my lovely heels helping you to trust every step."
"I'm so sorry, Miss Alexis. I know you must have others that need your time. I'm..."
She interrupted me, saying, "Baby, we all get lost in the dark. Although, not many of us get lost in a dark ass canyon in the middle of Utah at the end of October. I'll give you props for this backdrop."
I replied, "I thought I was prepared. I don't know what.."

"Honey, how could you be prepared when the Boy Scouts wouldn't honor your rainbow badge? You are in a river you chose, so trust the lesson she is offering."
I asked, "How do I do that? What's that even mean?"

She yelled, "G-A-B-G!!," as the echoes traveled the walls of the canyon.

I replied, "I get it. Get a Grip, Girl! I know your G-A-Double G chant well."

Miss Alexis said, "You clearly didn't listen, Brian. I said, "G-A-B-G, or Get a better God! "

I asked, "Get a bigger God?"

She laughed wildly, and she moved much closer to me, saying, "Oh Brian, you had me in stitches. I said, 'Get a better God!' Find a way to see God through a view you can trust and believe in, or you will always be a victim of every rising tide."

I replied, "You believe in God?"

Miss Alexis replied, "Oh yes! But don't worry. My way of seeing God is gorgeous. I guess the white guy with the long flowing beard with weirdly sensible shoes went out for a drink and never came back. He needed to move along, because his judgment was cramping my style."
I replied, "I must be having a very bizarre nightmare or an acid flash back."

She smiled and replied, "Honey, this canyon is real. This lesson is real, and it is finally sinking in that this moment is a far greater lesson about how you do life, Baby."

I asked, "How do I know this lesson won't kill me? I can't see and

I'm getting colder and colder."

"You're fine, except for the pickle you created by being in a canyon river with two thousand foot walls well past dark on a night with no moon in an area where they don't exactly love us gays. This is a plan that needed a plan. Do you feel me? Let's be honest. We all feel that way when we are in the lesson. Pain is always eroding the walls of our heart, so we can shine more brightly."

I replied, "That's easy for you to say. You seem like a drag queen who got trapped in a Hallmark store."

She looked shocked and then replied, "Girl, you can throw down some shade now. You used to just be a hyper carebear. Mother is proud."

I then pleaded with her, "Come on! You're not listening! How do I get out of here? Can't you just wave some magic wand and get me out of here?"

"Focus, my Dear! G-A-B-G! Clearly, the God you're working with isn't helping you to trust in this moment. So, get a better one!"

I asked, "Aren't you a God now? Why can't you just rescue me?"

Miss Alexis came closer now, "Some likely think I am, and really, they're right in some ways. I've been told I am a revelation, but I can honestly say that I am a part of God. We are all a part of God, even the ones the world cannot see yet or love yet."
I asked, "You mean people like us?"

"No Brian. I mean anyone the world judges for being who God made them to be. I know how hard that is for you to imagine, Baby. As gay people, we were told God hated us, so we learned to rely on one another as a family. Our backwards disco with our small stage that I always made large was our church. It's time to

put down the lie. God loves all of her children, Brian. "
I reply, "I hope you're right."

Miss Alexis grabbed my hands in her, and she said, "She loves each and every one of us, even the ones who spend so much time trying to tell the world God only loves them. It's crazy that Love creates more Love, and we treat it as a bank account. If I love everyone, how can there ever be enough? In truth, loving everyone ensures there is always enough."

"I love you, Miss Alexis."

She replied, "I love me too, Darling. Now, get your butt out of this river. The locals are going to find out there's a homo in this canyon, and that may not turn out well for you."

"Thank you, Sis."

She replied, "Always. Now, go out and make your life matter by making your life matter. The first step is the hardest, but you know I'm right there with you."

Then, she waved and her eyes welled with tears, but we both knew we would be together again.

The silence of that canyon was no longer frightening, and the darkness seemed to descend even more. I couldn't even see my hand in front of my face, and I felt my fear building again. I placed my hand on my heart, and I felt the river in a new way. I could trust the force of water pushing at my legs, and I knew I was heading in the right direction.

As I stood in this river, my pulse softened so my mind could begin to quiet the hamster wheel of fear controlling my cerebral cortex. Her soft force was now felt as a wall of gentle light pushing me through the steps of deep water going one step at a time, but she was always nudging me in the right direction.

The sound of the waterfall softened to a purr as my feet landed on the steps that took me back to the concrete pathway, where I barely made the final 9:45 P.M. shuttle back to the parking lot.

I will never forget the forces at play when I "came-out" as a gay man in 1987 at the ripe age of fifteen. As I opened that door to the colorful life that awaited me, one hand was embraced by the diverse rainbow of people who saved a seat for me at their table, and the other hand was embraced by Death. Almost every person I met during those formative years of my gay adventure has died.

I am a soul with far more time than so many of my beautiful teachers. I am growing old, but they are forever young.

My friend Scott Jackman, who was basically my Gay Godfather, used to say, "A good story should disturb the comfortable and comfort the disturbed." He also said the greatest gift to return the love to the previous generation is to teach what saved your ass on the darkest night of your soul, and it should always start with, "Thank you, God."

So, here's to a lineage of souls far wiser than me. My wisdom seems to always be earned in some manner, and more often than not, through making gigantic mistakes or moments when my focus on myself caused me to lose sight of my impact on all of you. We can justify so many things when our pain speaks louder than our purpose.

This book is for you, my dear companion. Your fear of not being good enough and not being sure if central office didn't make a mistake with you is your canyon. Mediumship is not about being enough. It is about caring so much for the suffering person in profound grief that your fear is required to take a backseat.

Shame is a pair of flats; Love is a pair of heels. Trust me. They will fit perfectly, because they were made for you.

Just don't get the shiny red ones on the top shelf and click them together, saying, "There's no place like home." They'll just lock you up for that.

Trust Spirit, even when you don't trust yourself.

There will be a moment when you will know you are participating in a miracle, and there will be a time when you will know that you are one.

Until that moment, please hold my hand and let's place a leaf in the water together.

I see you.

I believe you.

I cheer for you.

Now, onto the real work. Get your number two pencils sharpened and listen up! I'm going to drop some wisdom on you that you are free to embrace or reject. I am not your authority. Consider this an offering.

It is a letter of love to a fellow companion called to the same river.

Grace is the river, and the leaf is our prayer.

Love, Brian

P.S. - G-A-B-G, Bitches!! (From your Fairy Godmother Miss Alexis)

DEAR YOUNG MEDIUM,

Hello, my friend. In this sense, "young" does not indicate age. Rather, it reflects the call of mediumship and the ways in which we are all new to this journey. Each time we are participants in the sacred connection that occurs when a spirit reaches out to their loved one, we are truly changed. Death is the gentle hand that will embrace us when it is our time. Grief is often the invitation, and Love is often the way you found your "Yes." As you venture into this journey of the heart, you realize that mediumship is Love having the final say.

You had the courage to step forward and accept the call. You likely feel anxious and wonder if you are good enough or if you are truly a medium. I cannot answer that for you. I would recommend never placing that question in the hands of another person. This question belongs in the prayers and meadows of meditation with you and the world of Spirit. The answer is often there, but we seek the confidence of one we perceive as more seasoned or more established to offer us that answer.

This, for me, was the beginning of this journey. If the approval of others and the world was my goal (which it has been at times), my sense of stability in my calling was always determined by others. The inner weather report was reported to me in either the eyes of their judgment or the eyes of their approval. If I had earned their approval, then I needed more and more of it to get the winds of confidence high enough to continue in my work.

If I received the eyes of judgment or a weary apathy from a person I deemed as a mentor or teacher, then my expectation of them carrying the sun for me would plant me more firmly in the land of doubt. I wasn't trusting Spirit. Rather, I had given that role to a person, who would ultimately have no choice but to let me down at some point.

There is a call to go inward and to anchor ourselves more fully in our inner world as mediums. Without this, the opinion of others and our need for approval can completely take us off track.

In this moment, please place your hand on your heart and try this prayer,

> *I offer myself to you in Spirit. I am ready to be open and vulnerable to receive the messages of healing for your beloved. If they seek me for this connection, I will trust you are the light that guided us together. Whether you are a family member or a dear friend, I will open my heart to you so that your presence fills the space and guides the time we will share. Thank you for choosing me to be your communicator.*
>
> *I will offer my songs of fear and doubt to the wind, so that my presence is yours. My eyes, my ears, and my very heart are yours to sing through me the song of Love you have for this person across from me.*
>
> *As a medium, I am an instrument for you, so your love can have the final say. Thank you for this honor.*

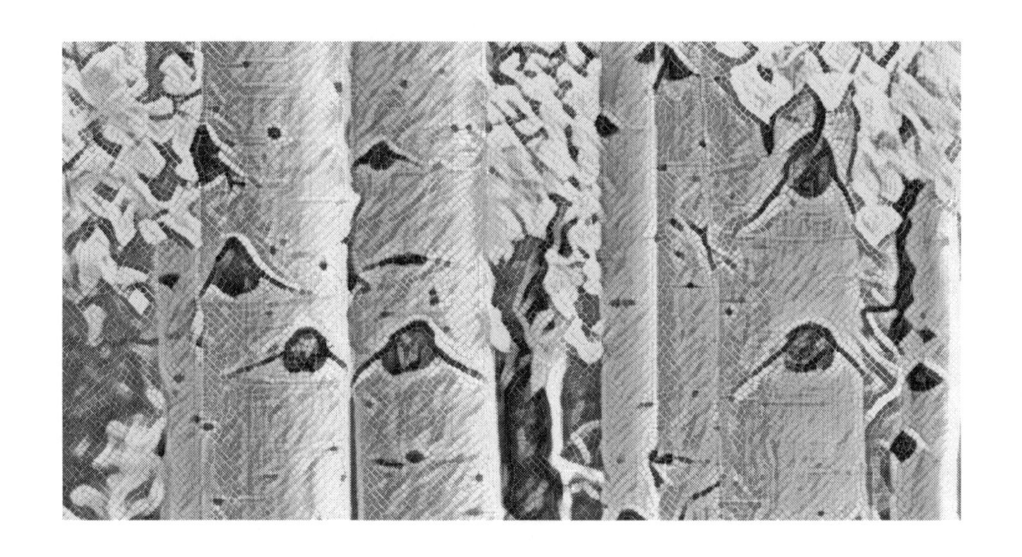

Lesson 1 - Mediumship Is A Lesson In Vulnerability And Trust.

Note: This story is not original. I heard this story in the rooms of a 12-step program for many years and I could not find a citation for it. I have created a new version of this tale, because the wisdom of this story has come to revisit me in some of the most important moments of my life. I hope you enjoy.

Imagine that God comes to town. Let's pretend it's a world tour with a proper light show and sexy back-up dancers. (Why can't she have backup dancers? It's my version of this old tale.) In my mind, she would be a grandmotherly figure with a hand-knit sweater that wraps around her body, but she curses like a sailor. Regardless of your ethnic background, you would see yourself in her skin, her eyes, her hair, and her presence. She would reflect all of us. You would know you belonged to her the moment you saw her, and she would feel like a family member.

Oh! And she comes into town on her lovely new bicycle. Yes, I said a bicycle, and it would have a lovely basket of course. As she steps off her bicycle, she stands in all her beauty in the center of the crowd. People scream, "We love you, God! We love you!" Then, she grabs the microphone saying, "It's Miz Goddess, please. Good morning, my Lovelies. Thank you for greeting me today. I have an invitation for all of you. Will you accept?"

The crowd screams, "Yes! We accept! Yes! Yes!"

She continues, "Okay. Let me start by saying I love you. I always have, even when you imagined I was far from you. I will prove this to you today."

Then, she snaps her fingers and a silver line of thread appears in the sky, from her feet all the way to the tallest mountain in the world.

Miz Goddess asks, "How many of you think I can ride my bicycle from here to the tallest mountain in the world?"

The crowd screams, "Yes. We believe! We believe! You can do anything!!!"

She looks at the crowd with sincere kindness and love as she receives everyone's love and approval.

Then, she looks at the crowd and says, "How lovely of all of you. Then, get in the basket."

Mediumship for me requires that I get in the basket for every client. This is not as easy as many people may imagine, because my mind tells me that I am not good enough and that I don't deserve this great responsibility or that maybe this time, it won't work. When I first awakened to this experience, I remember saying to my guides, "Why me? I'm a broken man with a history filled with the wreckage of all those I have hurt along the way. I am a self-centered wreck! There must be a mistake. There are others far better than me."

This is not false humility. The truth is that I had become very good at hating myself in multiple ways, and this calling to mediumship rocked my world. I still had the idea that God approved or disapproved of me, because I saw all love that way. I could not imagine another version of love, because I had never offered this love. I kept hearing my angels say, "Just get in the basket." Okay, so sometimes, they get irritated and they say, "Will you just get in the damn basket? We don't have all day!"

So, I stand in the light and trust. Every connection offers me new eyes, new ears, and a more open heart. Every spirit is teaching me to love all people and in turn, to love and forgive myself. For me, this is the gift of mediumship. The livelihood, the level of status one achieves, the approval and certifications one gains, and the fame that greets some of us are also lessons this journey offers. However, I believe that healing is the lasting gift and these lessons of love transform our souls.

All I am asked to do is to get in the basket. Easy, right? Ha! That's why I depend on my "soul anchors" as I like to call them—those special companions that hold your hand when it grows dark or when the path takes a sharp curve. Getting in the basket when a client is across from you questioning your authenticity, can feel like walking off a high dive and trusting there is a pool with actual water in it.

It is befriending this discomfort that, for me, has made the difference. I still feel the fear, but I completely trust that Spirit will always be there. Spirit has never let me down. My expectations are not always met in the way I imagined, but Spirit has never let me down. I am always moved by the surprises and turns a reading takes, offering far more than my wisdom ever could have offered.

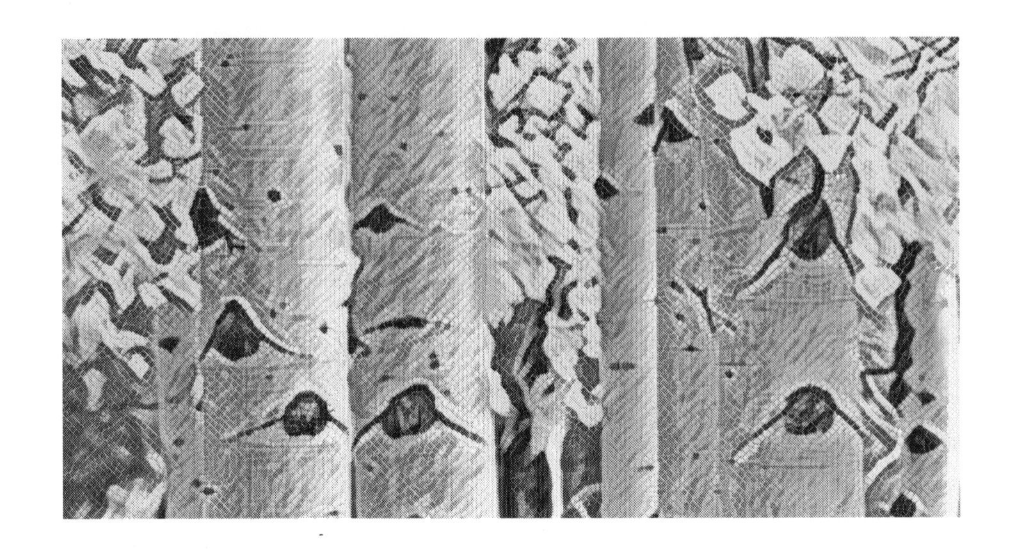

Lesson 2 - Mediumship Is About Companioning The Bereaved And Honoring The Journey Of Grief.

I've had some pretty moving experiences with spirits coming through in an impromptu way, especially when I was just starting on this journey. I didn't always have the best boundaries, but over time, I learned to simply ask permission if the setting protected the client's privacy.

One time, for example, we had hired a crew of painters to work in our home after getting some wainscoting done in our bedroom and bathrooms. After three days of the workers being in our house, I kept feeling the presence of a little girl. I said to Spirit that if I was meant to connect, they needed to create the space and time. I mentioned to the workers that I work as a medium, and encouraged them to ask any questions they might have. I opened the door wide and trusted the space would come if it was meant to be.

As I stood making lunch one day, the female painter—I'll call her Karen—came to get some water. We started chatting. I finally got the courage to ask her. I said, "Weird as this sounds, can I ask if you had a daughter pass? Around six years old?"

"Yes," Karen said. "Emma is her name. I was wondering if you would feel her."

I asked for permission and we connected with Emma for roughly thirty minutes. Karen's daughter had experienced significant disabilities while her spirit was here. The first thing I was asked to communicate for Emma was the basic "Thank you" sign from American Sign Language. That's how she'd let me know she had big physical challenges while she was here. When Emma was diagnosed with leukemia, she was five. Karen came to accept over time that Emma's journey would be cut short. Due to relationship issues, Karen became Emma's only parent when she was two. Emma showed me how Karen would place her in her car seat every day and use a strap wrapped with a sheepskin.

This mother was deeply bonded with her daughter, and I will

never forget the most significant moment of the reading for me. Emma told me to say, "Mommy, I can hold the stars in my hands! I can hold the stars in my hands!" I looked down and my hands were making a grabbing motion. My hands are often doing their own thing in a reading, and I sometimes see the link between what my hands are doing with the intended message. Often times, I don't.

The mother's reaction surprised me. Karen looked shocked. She covered her mouth with her hands, saying, "I can't believe this."

I asked, "Why is that so significant to you?"

"I placed glow-in-the-dark-stars on her ceiling two weeks before she died. I wanted her to know where she would be going. I told her to reach for them with her hands, and eventually, she would be able to hold the stars in her hands."

After my time with Karen, I recognized that our loved ones on the other side will always be connected to us.

Sometimes, spirit children who visit will come to me after a reading—it doesn't happen often but the experience is always moving. As I was working in the yard after the painters had gone home, Emma came to visit me. She said nothing, just danced and twirled around the yard, showing me how well she moves on the other side. I had been so upset after the reading, confused about why a beautiful soul would be locked in a body that required significant levels of care and allowed her little to no movement.

As I watched Emma dance, smiling joyfully, I recognized that once again, Spirit was offering me a lesson. Emma's body was the perfect vessel for the lessons she was offering us and for her own growth as a soul. Every challenge is always a lesson and an opportunity. As a consequence, I hold the idea of physical disability differently today.

Now, I look at loved ones caring for their family members with significant disabilities and I send them love. I recognize that a powerful soul is offering each and every one of their family members an opportunity to love in a more powerful and significant way.

I have connected now with quite a few children on the other side. I have even been blessed to experience the miracle of seeing a newborn soul enter the world and then blessed to see them complete their journey. As a former teacher and family therapist, I truly believe these children are teachers for all of us. When they leave us so soon, I believe strongly that we are offered a lesson around knowing how sacred and powerful our time here is.

Knowing this does not make the hurt easier or give me peace about these losses. The loss of a child is devastating for parents and family members. When I was a therapist, this type of loss felt cruel, without purpose—except, I thought, perhaps to just cause meaningless suffering.

Today, however, I believe these children remain deeply connected to their parents throughout their lives. I also believe these children are still bathed in the love of their parents and still learn and grow alongside their parents even when they are on the other side. The greatest difference is that the child is free from the boundaries their bodies created for them.

Karen, the painter who had lost her daughter, Emma, spent six years of her life addicted to methamphetamines and alcohol—all to deal with the pain of her daughter's death. Her addiction brought her to the very edge of life, where she had even been homeless. When I met her, she had just received her one-year AA coin for sobriety. Her daughter and her angels worked hard to ensure that Karen (always a mother) knew that Emma was still deeply connected to her.

For me, I choose to believe the love Karen poured into Emma while she was here was being returned to her from the other side. Karen is nothing less than a miracle and a teacher. She chose to live again in the face of terrible, painful circumstances. She chose to hope again, to believe that her story was still being written. That's a level of faith and courage that continues to teach me, even now.

We, as mediums, are invited into hard places with people. Even as the loved one in spirit guides us and provides meaningful evidence along the way, we are also left with our other role in this process – the compassionate and loving witness. We join with people in that space and tell the truth. We don't walk away from the horror of that moment or seek to make someone feel better by offering platitudes. We witness and we tell the sincere truth of what information is offered. However, at the end of a reading, our soul has an opportunity to offer compassion, love, and sincere empathy.

Depending on where they are in their journey of grief, I seek to offer some guidance around the stages of loss. For example, with a new loss, I share with people that often times, it takes six to nine months for the shock to lift. I let them know that they may be surprised that at nine months or a year after a death, the feelings and thoughts can be much harder. By preparing them, they can be gentle with themselves if this becomes their experience. The world often expects that we are ready to rejoin the world at six months, and often times, the heart of the grief journey is just beginning.

The best salve for a grieving heart is often an acknowledgement of their suffering and honoring that the journey of grief does not obey timelines or follow the expectations the world around us may have. Our grief honors our capacity to love, so treating grief as an illness further isolates the suffering. People will slowly withdraw parts of their hearts if we do not grow in our capacity to hold space and honor the grieving heart.

Mediumship and grief are companions in this work. When we are focused solely on evidence and seeking validation of our skills in the work, we may lose sight of the critical role grief plays in the work. People contact us because they are often suffering and seeking some sense of ground in the storm. As dramatic as that sounds, I have found this to be the case. Beyond the evidence, we are witnesses of great suffering and profound sadness. The more we normalize and honor the way grief speaks to the client, the more potential we create for their loved one to offer their hope and healing through us.

* * *

I want to be the soft hand for the suffering when it appears, but I must also accept that hand when I need the support.

My mother died after a long journey with dementia and other health issues in a nursing home almost two years ago. In the months to follow, three dear friends would also die. I lived in a cocoon of sadness, shock, anger, frustration, guilt, and my feet were frozen in a river of shock. My emotions were tidal, and they were mostly in the distance and unable to be felt or acknowledged. Then, my little guy Nash, a 7 lb. toy poodle we rescued from a puppy mill eight years prior, also died in my arms as the veterinarian finally calmed the storm of Cushing's Disease. Nash had lost all of his back hair and had a desire to eat that could never be satisfied. He was inconsolable, as the tumor on his kidney forced his body to release a toxic amount of Cortisol.

These losses devastated me.

I thought being a medium and knowing that death is a transition would save me from the chaos of that storm, but I was drowning. The very words I had said to others were not keeping my head above water. Instead, I was meeting a different iteration of an old lesson – doubt. Doubt had the upper hand in this battle at times, and I would struggle to get out of bed or to answer the phone. It got real, it got dark, and it got painful as hell.

This was a season of loss, and I was wrecked.

I promised I wouldn't write in a way that made the hard parts seem easy. I hope by me telling the truth, that others who find themselves in these dark places will see part of their story in this tale.

I have had to honor that my own grief invites me to allow the warm blanket of hope and purpose to embrace me once again. I am here and doing this life. I am not above the lessons nor am I impenetrable to the pain of life. I don't get to escape any of it. I actually believe that's what makes us good at this work, because we are not in any way above the people we serve.

We are companions in this journey of loss, and we are witnesses to the miracles that occur when a person opens their heart to their loved ones in a new way.

If you know what the wallpaper in hell looks like, come sit with me. Your hurt, your sadness, your anger, your guilt, your hopelessness, and your frustration no longer frighten me. You think you are dying and will never feel the light of the sun again on your face, but I know that you are being reborn out of the ashes of this moment.

I know you are becoming the love in the world you desperately need.

You will know how to be a companion to another in this fire, and learning to witness and offer grace to another will somehow quiet the searing heat of your loss. Mediumship, for me, has been the very process by which I have learned to heal in the face of so many losses.

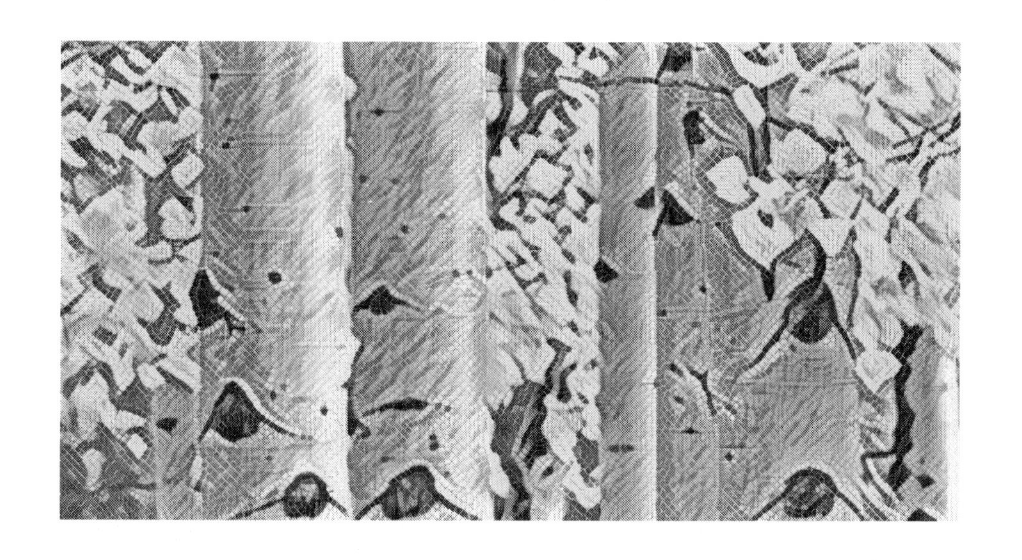

Lesson 3 - Mediumship Is An Ability And Not A Gift.

Mediumship is an ability, and like any ability, we are given the opportunity to learn and grow from every exchange. If we forget we are students, that is when we can cause the greatest harm. This has been true for me in my work. There is always a way back, a way to redeem ourselves, if we have the courage to hold up the mirror. Otherwise, we may be awake to the hidden unconscious needs of our clients while being completely in the dark about ourselves.

I don't believe, as some mediums express, that our ability will be taken from us if we are not aligned in positive ways. That's a bit too puritanical for me. If this work was about being worthy, then I wouldn't be included. The guides that accompany me understand that I am a soul in progress, and that I am here to fail and mess up a lot. Otherwise, what would their work be? Besides, they are there to love me as I grow towards the ideals of this work. I keep them busy. Hopefully, my guides get good insurance and paid holidays. Trust me. They need it and they certainly deserve it.

The beliefs we create around our work should be questioned. Do these beliefs give me authority over another person or make it seem that I know more about life than they do? Do I pretend to be a guru who has wisdom surpassing all human understanding? Do I step into a reading assuming that if I had the backpack of their issues, I would know exactly what they should do to improve their life? Confidence is not the same as arrogance.

We are invited into sacred spaces where suffering meets purpose. When we witness these moments and honor the challenges clients are facing, we are given a chance to empower the client who has all of the inner wisdom they need. Most confusion we have in life protects us from needing to take action. The fear of making significant changes sometimes encourages us to set up a lawn chair in the park of confusion, because we need the pause to build the confidence and support networks to step into action.

Do we create beliefs that serve to make others' spiritual gifts feel small? Does our certification or training with a certain teacher make our opinions or professional standing have more weight than others? I've found that at the end of the day, the world won't care about those things. It is always the quality of reading you offer and the demonstration of love and respect you extend to each client that carries the day. No amount of pretty websites and fancy words will rescue the reputation of a medium who is selling a story about their ability they can't honor.

I'm embarrassed that I didn't always know this, and that the early experiences in my mediumship and the positive comments I received became my narrative for the quality of work I offered. My ego started to sing more loudly than my soul. I was unaware of my limitations in this work, and I confused the world with what I was actually able to offer.

Here's an example of how this showed up in my work:

EMAIL FROM A FATHER

> **You have been sent here by God and anointed with a blessed gift. I must know how to best ensure my soul will be allowed to enter the doors of Heaven. I know this may sound crazy, but I'm so worried about this. Can you please tell me how to know I will be worthy? Can we connect weekly, so my daughter can tell me how to proceed?**

In this moment, this father who is a devout Catholic, is asking me by email about how to ensure his soul will be saved. His daughter died from suicide, and her body wasn't found for months after her disappearance in her small town where she had attended college. They discovered her body in the spring, and it was clear that her death had been a suicide. The father had been in grief counseling for over a year, and he couldn't shake the idea he was being punished for her death.

In this moment, I had a choice. Do I allow the belief that I'm some highly evolved being sent by God to prevail? Or, do I honor my truth that I am as human as anyone else and imperfect as everyone else. This father was incredibly vulnerable, and his reading gave him some impressions of me that gave me a lot of unearned authority with him. In the wrong hands, this vulnerability could be used to deepen someone's pocketbook and also create great harm with a person who is in profound grief.

There is a vulnerability our clients carry in the turbulent waters of grief that needs to be honored. If we forget this, we can cause undue harm.

When questions like this come my way, I often have a client place their hand on their heart and ask for guidance from their understanding of the Divine. Because I see mediumship as an ability, I recognize that in that moment, my response matters. I can choose to empower and companion, or I can create a lasting legacy of hurt. He needed to understand that as a medium, I know I am not special or above another soul. The client needed to understand that he can access the Divine in his own way that works for him, and most importantly, he needed to recognize his daughter in spirit was available to him. He only needed to practice trusting this connection and allow it to evolve over time. If I deny this client that connection and create a dependency because he believes mediums are the only people able to connect and feel the presence of their loved ones, then I have created a prison of belief that will cause harm for him from that day forward.

This, for me, is the foundation of all ethics in our work. If we believe we are anointed ones or any other nonsense that places us above our fellow souls, we are learning a lesson where the consequences are often paid by the most vulnerable. We must work together to assist one another in this aspect of our development, so we are always the companion to the suffering and never the authority.

Lesson 4 - We Are All Mediumistic Even Though We May Not All Be Mediums.

We don't actually need mediums. Many people go through their grief journeys beautifully without that support. I worked for many years in hospice, and I was blessed to observe many people finding their own ways to connect meaningfully with their loved one who had died. They felt them, they saw them, or they had a dream that their loved one had come to visit. In the counseling room, people would share many experiences like this.

We often did an activity called "Letter to a Loved One." The bereaved person would come to the session having written a letter to their loved one. I would surprise them at the session by having them read the letter out loud and then write a response from their loved one to the letter. We'd light a candle and clients would fill most of the sixty minutes with the words and thoughts of their loved one. We'd also do an "empty chair" activity where the client would sit opposite an empty chair. They would picture their loved one sitting across from them. They would speak to their loved one and then switch chairs and speak as their loved one in response. It's a powerful activity, and I believe that every time we did this, their loved one was there, honored to hear their own words emerging from the mouth of their loved one.

I remember hearing Marc's name cross my lips for the first time after he died. A dear friend and I were hiking in the woods. She and I were doing a three-day backpacking trip. On our second day in the woods, she asked me if I had lost anyone to AIDS. It was so nonchalant that I wasn't sure how to answer. She didn't likely realize how big of a door to my past she was opening. For many miles and many curves on a winding trail, I told the story of Marc. It was the first time I had used his name so many times in one conversation. She gently offered kind encouragements that were sometimes words and sometimes soft verbal responses, letting me know she was hearing every word. It resulted in a final moment in an aspen grove with blazing golden colors where she held me as I cried. It felt as if I had finally been seen with that loss for the first time. She was the witness. She never once pulled the story onto her path in any way.

She listened with presence. She created a container for healing I will never forget. My backpack became lighter and lighter with every passing footstep. Marc was present in every one of those moments. His eyes, his face, the way he held my hand, his words, and our memories filled that forest with every pressed footprint along the path. No one was the medium, but this was a very mediumistic experience.

His presence washed over me and left me with a peace I had never felt with his loss. I knew he was okay, and I was finally feeling that I might be okay too. Okay is a big step in the journey of grief, and it took a witness.

For me, mediumship is just one of the ways for our loved ones to connect with us. It is not the only way, and I try to empower clients in this wisdom so they don't develop a dependency on me or perceive that I am the only person able to connect with their loved ones. I believe my job is to prove this communication exists and then seek to empower clients to begin to nurture that connection with their loved one on the other side. I know we offer a very powerful service, but our loved ones in spirit belong to our story. A client's experience with their beloved in spirit will always be more powerful than one we offer.

We can create the space for this to occur and for this connection to deepen and grow, but we are the witnesses. We witness spirit, and the information flows. We also witness the client, and we honor the courage it requires to step forward on the path of life without the human presence of their loved ones. We don't take away grief, because we don't dishonor love. Knowing our purpose in this work can assist us greatly in knowing how to best serve the suffering soul in grief, because, indeed, we are not separate from this experience.

We, too, are passengers in the river of grief. We, too, know the hurt and blessing grief offers. It is often the very experience of our grief that opened our hearts fully to this calling. Who knows what doors grief will open in another's life? As a medium, your grief is what allows you to connect with the vulnerability, the grace, the perseverance, the courage, and the presence to serve every client that comes to your door.

The river of grief is tidal, and the rapids can rise at times when we are ill prepared for the emotions and memories those waves carry to our feet. We are all in the river of grief together, and we begin to trust the way we need our own witness when we suffer. As grief erodes the hurt, the pain, the anger, the loss, then we are often left behind with a peace and a sense of renewed connection to our beloveds.

We know grief is recursive and deepens over time, and our loved ones in Spirit are our greatest guides in this journey. This awareness serves us in other ways too. When we recognize that a loved one in the light is guiding them, we no longer feel responsible for the client in ways that could disempower them and overwhelm us. We trust that Spirit has a plan for every client, and that we are not in the role of fixing broken people. Grief never shows us that we are broken; it always teaches us that we are whole.

A grace joined me in those waters that has forever redefined my faith. Every loss is an opportunity for the heart to be comforted by the light and to become a more powerful expression of that light. Suffering serves a purpose, even if we are unable to fully honor the value while we're in it. Without this experience, I doubt any of us would have ever said "Yes!" to this calling.

If a client walks away from a reading completely focused on how amazing you are as a medium, that will not transform their life. If a client walks away knowing that their loved ones are still with them, this awareness will transform their life. The love and companionship of the Divine is available to each and every one of us.

While some may work professionally as mediums, all of us can feel the warm embrace of Spirit's love. A mother can always place her hand on her heart and feel the love of her son wash over her in Spirit.

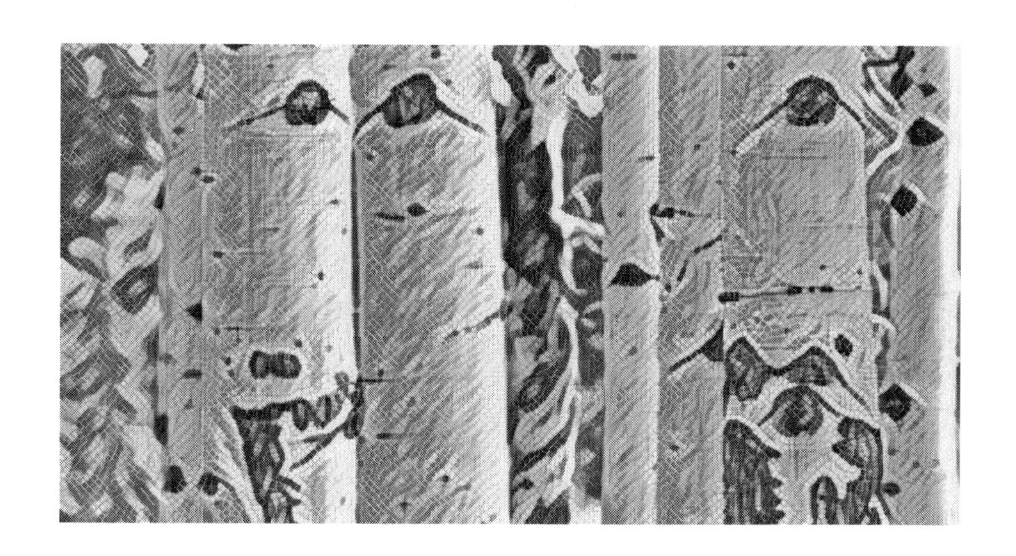

Lesson 5 - Mediumship Should Protect The Vulnerability Of Every Client.

I hate learning lessons. I'm not a super evolved being that often approaches the lessons of mediumship or life always with an open heart and mind. I'm owning this at the outset, because this work requires self-reflection in a manner unique to any field serving other humans.
Maybe in my next life, I'll have flowers in my hair and say things like, "I'm dancing in the fire of my truth and feeling the wings of spirit flow in my chakras." More often, my inner dialogue sounds like, "Well Bowles, you screwed the pooch on that one! That was reckless and self-centered."

I know I need to work on being gentler with myself and I'm committed to that, but I must own with all of you that I have caused harm in this work at times. To be of service to a fellow soul who is suffering, I want to take a better account of the ways in which I get in the way of being compassionate and decent. The person reaching out to me for a reading is often called "the sitter", and that reminds the medium that our central focus is meant to mainly be on the loved ones in the light who are there to offer hope and evidence of their connection that surpasses even death.

I sometimes forget the beautiful and vulnerable client that had the courage to say "Yes!" to chatting with a middle-aged D-homosexual claiming to be able to chat with dead people. (Yes, the D- was an official evaluation performed by the LGBTQ Council for North America, and my evaluation was peer reviewed.). I've been ordered to listen to more drag queen anthems and to wear only a rainbow flag on Sundays. I don't think it's working.

There was a mother who reached out to me asking for a reading and her simple request was to do this with me in person.

Because of my health challenges and me being between two places, I encouraged her multiple times to just do it by phone or reach out to another medium. She kept saying, "I know you're the person for me." So, I was supposed to reach out to her when I was back in Colorado to set up our time and I conveniently forgot, because I saw her as demanding and her simple request became too inconvenient for me. She called me while in Colorado and said, "You're home and I've waited a long time. Is there any way we can connect this week?"

I finally relented and set the time for us to meet.

When she entered my home, this lovely mother entered my home and immediately, the energy changed. My dogs could not get close enough to her. And, I felt nothing but joy and gratitude for her presence. Her son came through beautifully, and he had been murdered by two men with guns in a drug exchange. She identified his body at the morgue in a cold manner even a TV procedural drama would avoid. That was the last moment she had with her baby boy. She touched his hair to try to move it from his forehead and kissed his cheek. She didn't have enough money to do the burial she desired, so she agreed to cremation.

At the end of our time, the mother asked if she could hug me. As we embraced, she wept and wept and wept. She said, "I can feel him. I can really feel him."

I got it. She needed that moment. She didn't care about the artful details he provided or that I got his age wrong and I offered no name. She needed the embrace. She understood that his energy was blending with mine and she needed a different goodbye. I was intent on doing it by phone. I put her off far longer than was necessary and lacked follow through. She knew it needed to be in person, and I balked and made that simple request the reason for not getting her addressed thoughtfully and soon.

As I walked her to the car, she said, "Thank you for your time. I was afraid you didn't want to meet with me." Ouch! In that moment, I realized that she wasn't the sitter. She was the other Spirit. A medium is holding the light between both souls. She was just as important as the Spirit, because she is too a spirit. I will never work with a sitter again, only a client.

I failed to honor the vulnerability of the person in profound grief. I'm a big believer that until I own it, I cannot grow from it. It's painful to see how my self-centered demands of clients or my lack of consideration for their level of vulnerability caused harm.

Lesson 6 - Mediumship Is A Reliable Force Of Love.

I have a serious health issue, so I spend a lot of waking hours in doctors' offices being offered new prescription drugs to address the daily challenges of having a brain recklessly parked on the curb of my spinal cord. My cerebellum got drunk one night and crashed into the top of my spine, where it remains cramped against the spinal cord, blocking spinal fluid and causing nerves to scream for release. This accident scene offers some challenges at times, and new medicines often have unique side effects. When you're an ADHD kinda fella like me, it seems most side effects operate in opposite or goofy ways.

I always call my good friend Angel when stuff like this pops up for me. Angel is my sister who has stunning silver gold dreadlocks, and she sometimes describes herself as a woman and sometimes as a man. I use the pronoun "she", because she told me that she mostly relates to the "she" part of herself in this life.

Angel makes me touch way too many trees during hikes and has me hold certain stones during our walks until I have a quiet enough energy to not irritate her. Yup, we're talking a Super Hippie! You can't get hippier than her. She also wears essential oils that result in no insect or bug wanting anything to do with her, but it must have a negative impact on her love life. It is not a "come hither" kinda smell. I never feel like removing my clothes and popping on a Sade CD when I'm near her. I more feel like we're heading for a super shaman gathering where the demons don't stand a chance.

Angel also suffers from a rough seizure disorder, and she has a pretty solitary life like me, except when she's traveling the nation doing healings and teachings about mystical rocks. I called her my Forest Shaman Goddess of the Rocks in my typical frantic and urgent way, hoping she could guide me through these turbulent waters of US pharmaceuticals. As she answered the phone, I skipped all of the niceties and held my prescription in my hands. The white bag and stapled booklet warning me of the all of the dangers to my kidneys and liver over time glared at me, as the sticker with the open mouth reminds me to eat with that medicine. The sticker looks like it is screaming, so I do exactly that as I yell into the phone,

"Angel! I need your help! The doctor put me on a new medicine. Should I take it?!?"
Angel replies in her soft and gentle tone, "Did your doctor prescribe those medicines?"
"Yes, but with my mediumship, I know these drugs, especially steroidal drugs, can really impact my ability. I don't want to damage my ability in any way, and I want to ensure I..."
Angel interrupts with the short nanosecond of air I offered her, saying, "Brian, your doctor prescribed these medicines. Do you trust this doctor?"
"Yes, she's been with me for a long time. I do trust her. She saved me from the nasty brain surgery the other doctor wanted to do."
Angel replied, "Maybe, Spirit had something to do with getting the right doctor for you. Do you think that could be true?"

This is where every conversation eventually lands with me reciting the phrase, "Yes, that makes sense" as I nod my head repeatedly.

Then, she surprised me and taught me one of the most powerful lessons regarding mediumship.
"Brian, do you think your mediumship is fragile? Do you see it as being very fragile and must have the perfect conditions to work?"

I said nothing.

"Well Bri, we'll call that answer affirmative. That doesn't make much sense, does it? Our mediumship is the strongest part of us, meant to work and serve us under the harshest of conditions. Remember that this connection saved your life as a child when your world was unpredictable and scary. Isn't that true?"

"Yes." This part of our talks was where I had nothing more to offer, except my agreement. She was clearly the wiser of the two of us, even though she'd never admit it. She continued with a statement that I repeat to myself whenever a person is calling for their reading and I'm not at my best. I'm no longer afraid I won't be able to connect, because that fear has died.

"Brian, your mediumship is the stone in the river not the floating leaf. No matter the rush of the river, your mediumship is steadfast and unshakable."

I replied, "That makes sense. I've never thought of it that way."

"Brian, one day, you will recognize that Spirit loves you in this way. Spirit is there for us as the stone in the river of life. We can always count on her strength and she will never abandon us, no matter the circumstances. It is our job to trust in this and become more and more like this for those we love and especially those we don't."

"Yes." Yes. I knew she was right. She's basically Yoda but stunning.

"Maybe, it's time to look at all of your rules for what makes mediumship work and reconsider this list. Is that list trusting Spirit or is it conditions you've created that aren't real? You really think Spirit doesn't want you to take a steroid medicine that reduces swelling on the back of your brain so you can function more effectively in the world?"

"No."

"Spirit's love has no conditions, except the ones we create. We do this with living people too, and then we make these conditions real. Love just is. The birds who migrate across the planet have no conditions. They trust. The plant bulbs I place in the Earth every fall have no conditions. They rise in perfect timing with the seasons, because they trust. Mediumship will always be about trust and never the conditions of fear we create. When you know this, your mediumship will no longer feel like a weather report changing with the afternoon winds."

"Angel, what do you mean by mediumship being a stone in the river? I always think of our communication in mediumship as a flow that you surrender completely to, so the loved one in the light can be honored."

"You are describing two different things: we must know our role and know we are connected to the stone in the river, because the rise and fall of every story is emotional and intense. The loved one in the light is actually the water. Their essence and their stories wash over us, don't they? We are anchored, so we can hold this space and trust fully the loved one to reveal the story of their heart and the message for their beloved. If we remember we are held tightly to the stone, then we are steadfast and we anchor to our place with solid feet. We are not fragile and floating above the water. We are anchored and solid, so the loved one in the light can trust us to share their essence and their message of healing."

I replied, "Is it my drama-queen-ness that causes me to block mediumship?"

"Brian, I won't laugh at this one. You are a child of God, no less and no more than any other. We are all afraid, but mediumship is a surrender to trusting that we are not alone and we are loved. That's not an easy thing after living so much of our life feeling so alone. Can you offer yourself some grace here?"

I replied once again, "Yes. I've always considered myself the leaf on the water and seen this interaction as fragile and unreliable."

"Most mediums do. Most think mediumship is about attainment as other human accomplishments are. Mediumship is always asking us to trust more deeply the lessons life offers us. Most growth with Spirit is removing the conditions you placed there. I think of spiritual growth as removing jackets until you are light and free."

I understood the big idea, but I knew that part of this was out of my reach.

"Can you give me an example, Angel?"

She replied, "If you were to ask every medium in the world how they create their link, you will notice that some create big fences they have to climb every time they want to connect with Spirit. If you think about this, it's pretty insane. Some must meditate for an hour on their heads while doing three yoga poses in their third eye. We make the natural completely unnatural. Mediumship is a natural connection that has always been there. It is now that people are honoring this connection in their conscious mind. It doesn't mean we don't nurture this connection or have a meaningful process with intention for creating a link. Rather, it means we begin to acknowledge that this connection is natural and there for us through all moments of life."

I asked, "So, if we know we are anchored in the river of light, what does it mean to grow in our work? How do we attain this fully?"

Angel laughed, and then she said, "Brian, you care so much about accomplishment. How many certifications will hang on your wall until you know you were the right person to stand in that river for a person who is suffering? That is your journey."

I joined with her laughter, and I recognized a big truth for me. I'm always trying to build a resume that proves I have value and that I have something to offer, because I don't fully know I am loved or that I am enough as I am. How many frames will be enough?

Angel ended with, "I liked this chat we had today. It's a good reminder for me. You know, there are so many folks doing beautiful work as mediums that hate themselves. They are in the river of light experiencing miracles and healing for their clients, but they don't allow themselves the love that flows through them. Try this exercise for me, Bri."

"Oh great! Now, I've got another exercises to fail at," I joked.

"Brian, sometimes your sense of humor reveals that you don't love yourself. Maybe, you will one day know that you carry God's love to so many and it's not just by being a medium. It is that beautiful heart."

"Thanks Angel. I don't feel that..."

"Let's not build your drama. Let's instead get quiet and feel a different truth. Brian, when you know that the stone of mediumship is actually God's profound love for you, you will begin to feel wrapped in her waves and her light every time you do a reading. You will know that river is the voice of the souls who have passed, but that rock is the glowing heart of God that will never fail you. You're included in the love that passes through you. Don't you know this, Brian?"

I can honestly say this question haunts me at times. I often feel like a bad person trying to be a good person in this dance of mediumship. I often see it as a form of making amends for my past self-centered ways and the hurt I created.

But, the lesson of knowing God's love is the unshakable rock in the river has changed me as a medium. More than that, it is changing me. Maybe, these aren't different in any way.

Can I be with the glowing heart of God and allow that love to sustain me?

Lesson 7 - Mediumship Is A Healing Journey.

When I first began my work as a special education teacher, I was assigned to teach middle school mathematics (grades 6-8) to students who really struggled. We used games and story-telling adventures, where the students would use mathematics to advance the character in the story. We had a great time, but there was one student in my fourth period class, right before lunch, that was a true pain in the butt. He was always getting other students off task, saying the stories were lame, and throwing spit wads at his friends. They were so gross! One day, a spit wad even dropped from the ceiling onto my head and it was the nastiest luggie in the world.

I'd had enough. I went up to him at lunch, and I let him know he was no longer allowed to attend the field trip to the Denver Museum of Nature and Science. After telling our administrator, Harold Bolton, my decision, he very politely said, "Now Mr. Bowles, Ian will be joining you. Field trips are not rewards. They are learning experiences. He didn't do something worthy of being suspended."

I replied, "Now listen, he is not a child I would ever feel safe bringing into the community. He never listens. He is out of control." Harold then stood up and placed his knee on his chair. He leaned into me across his desk and said, "So, have you given up on Ian? Have you?"

I replied, "Definitely not. You don't get it, do you?" He looked kindly at me as he always did, saying, "Now Brian, Ian is a complicated kiddo. Have you read his file yet? I've suggested you do this twice. Have you?"

I replied, "No. A teacher's life is busy, so reading one kid's file from the counseling center is a big time issue." Harold replied, "He is going on the field trip with the other kids, and I guess you need to figure out what he needs from you and the other adults to be successful."

Ian went on the field trip, and it was completely insane!!! As our middle school students stood in line waiting to enter the Imax Theater at the group entrance, Ian broke a glass stink bomb. It had a strong smell of ammonia and rotten eggs. It was freaking awful, and the first-grade group in line with us began to cry and scream. It was my worst day of teaching ever by a long shot. Ian smirked as the entire group fell apart, and we were forced to leave early by the security staff. They arrested Ian, and he was taken to a local juvenile detention center for further evaluation. Ian looked so defeated, and I was grateful he was finally getting the consequence he deserved. I remember seething with anger the entire bus ride back to school, because I had been right. I knew this juvenile delinquent had no place in our school.

After doing my dramatic reenactment in Harold's office and enjoying the fact that this field trip had gone exactly as I had promised it would, Harold had me sit across from him in the comfy chairs where he normally met with parents. He said, "Are you done with your story?"

I replied with great admiration for myself, "Yes, I believe I am." If it was a court room, the jury would convict.

He then, in his plaintive and gentle manner, got more serious than I had ever seen him. He said, "Brian, you let me down. You didn't do what I asked, and now Ian is in danger of being placed in foster care." I felt punched in the stomach. I said, "Harold, I don't understand. I didn't think he should go. Aren't these natural consequences?"

Harold paused and looked at me with anger in his eyes. I had never in my life seen this look, and it stopped my defense. Harold asked, "Did you read his file and meet with the counselor to learn about Ian?" I quietly replied, "No."

Harold replied, "Then, you didn't do your job. You didn't prepare for him to be successful at all. You ensured he would fail."

Then, Harold pointed to the door, and he said, "You need to make this right. You will have a substitute tomorrow, and you will be charged a personal day. You spend tomorrow researching him and seeing if you have what it takes to help him, or I'll seek to have you transferred to another school. I need teachers who love these kids enough to see the story behind the story."

This is a very embarrassing story, because it's true.

I finally did the research. I was in the counseling office all day and I devoured everything I could to defend how right I was, but every page destroyed my position and my fundamental approach to being his teacher. His file looked like a first draft for "War and Peace." It was full of educational reports and psychological studies. Through the educational reports and years of meetings, a story emerged. It was the story behind the story.

Ian was living with his grandmother who had diabetes. Her diabetes had become so severe, that she had both of her feet amputated. She required significant care. She was tied to her wheelchair, and they lived in affordable housing in a one-bedroom apartment. Ian's grandmother was also diagnosed with congestive heart failure, and she was soon to be placed in the care of hospice.

Prior to being with his grandmother, Ian had experienced profound loss and abandonment. Because Ian's father had died from an overdose when he was three years old, Ian lived with his mother in San Diego, California. His mother had a serious addiction to heroine, and she was often using motel rooms that changed frequently to exchange her body for money to maintain her habit. Ian's address and schools changed so often many of the records of his first five years of school were simply impossible to locate. In addition, Ian had a serious issue with attending school. One report indicated that he missed more than seventy-percent of the days in a six-month period.

The reason Ian offered the psychologist in his third grade report for why he didn't attend school was that he was worried about his mother. He didn't understand why she couldn't come to school with him. Ian had witnessed many different men treat his mother in horrific ways. So, he never attended with any regularity, and they finally ended up in truancy court. In the third month of his fourth grade year when he had just turned eleven, the mother decided she could no longer handle the stress and oversight of the local social services office. So, she gave him fifty bucks and put him on a bus to head to Denver to live with his grandmother, her mother. His mother told him it was a birthday gift, and that he would only be there for a couple of weeks. Ian never saw or heard from his mother again.

Ian and his grandmother, Rosie, got along for some reason, and they both liked cop shows and reruns of the Lucille Ball show. They laughed and became bosom buddies. Ian fit in immediately and they created their own sense of family. As his grandmother became more and more fragile due to her diabetes, Ian picked up the slack and they became even closer through her multiple doctor's visits and hospitalizations. Ian even took the classes with her on how to eat right with diabetes, and he became the main cook for both of them. Ian was said to have become one heck of a cook with the support of her home-based aid worker and weekend classes in cooking. He wanted to be a chef one day. Ian still struggled with school, and he was often perceived as a challenging student.

In early December of his sixth-grade year, Ian and his grandmother received a call from the police department in the San Francisco Bay area, letting them know his mother's body had been found after a likely drug overdose. I received Ian as a student in the fall of his seventh-grade year, not even a year since the death of his mother.

So, the student I had identified as a delinquent was going through an unspeakable loss, and all I had to offer him was my judgment. My judgment didn't make the situation better. It only furthered the story for Ian that the world outside the four walls of his grandmother's place was cruel and unforgiving.

It was the last line in the psychological report that would quiet my judgment forever.

Final Quote from 5th Grade Psychological Report: Ian presents as a positive person with a maturity well above his peers on all relational testing and my own clinical assessment. It appears that his main reason for behavioral outbursts always has to do with the desire to be at home to protect his grandmother.

Ian returned to school five days later with the charges dropped. Harold was masterful at getting the authorities to see a softer way to address situations with children. He would always say, "We forget they are children when we are angry with them, because it allows us to justify our unwillingness to see the real need their behavior is begging us to see."

I finally got it. The trip to the museum took him too far away from the grandmother he was trying to protect.

As Ian entered my classroom before school started for us to discuss the event, I saw a completely different student in front of me. I noticed he hadn't bathed, and I saw that his jacket was way bigger on him than it should be.

"Ian, I need to start by telling you how sorry I am. I've been a complete jerk. I feel that we don't know one another well, and that's going to change. Can you tell me what happened for you at the museum?"

Ian moved back in his chair with his arms folded over his chest. Ian said, "Mr. B, I didn't mean to be so difficult that day. I know what I did was wrong."

I said, "Can you tell me what happened? What led you to.. you know?"

He replied, "Drop a stink bomb and make a bunch of children cry?

I'm not sure. It seemed funny in my head, but I never meant to hurt anyone."

"What did you learn?," I asked.

"I don't honestly know. I'd never drop a stink bomb again in a closed area."
I replied, "Well, that's a start."

"Mister B, I know what I did was wrong, and I feel really bad. Have you ever done something and you don't see any way to make it right?"

I replied, "Yes, Ian. I certainly know that feeling. Can you tell me why you really did it?"

Ian squirmed in his seat, and I almost rescued him from this dissonance, but then he blurted out, "I know you don't like me! I didn't even want to go, because I hate being in your class. It's obvious you hate me." Insert the dagger in my heart.

Ian was just beginning to tear up, and I looked right at him, saying, "Ian, I don't hate you. I need to show you I mean that. I know I have failed you in this way. You deserved so much more."

Ian looked at me and unfolded his arms, "I'm sorry, Mister B. I didn't expect you to really listen. It kinda confuses me."

I replied, "I'm mad at myself and I know I let you down."

Ian smiled for the first time since I'd met him, saying, "That's how I felt Mister B! That's how I feel!"

I said, "You know, Ian. I'm the adult in this situation, and this is really on my shoulders. Can you let me take this one?"

"Even adults screw up, Mister B. I think we all do. But, I threw the stink bomb? Not you. Don't be so hard on yourself. I've been going through some things."

I replied, "I'd really like to hear more about those things when you are ready."

Ian looked me right in the eye for the first time, and he said, "Mister B, why are you being so nice to me?"

I replied, "Because you are a hero pretending to be the villain. Everything you do is to make your grandmother's life better. I want to help with that. Does that make any sense?"

He looked over at me and looked incredulous, but then he nodded.

Then, the middle schooler energy picked up, and his leg started to shake.
Ian replied, "Yes, but if I'm honest, I thought I would get expelled."

I asked, "Did you hope to be expelled?"

"No, but maybe a part of me did. I'm used to teachers hating me, and I know I'm a bad kid. I don't even know why I'm such a jerk."

I replied, "You listen, Ian. I don't ever want to hear those words again. We have a lot in common, you and I. Will you give me another chance? I know I have to earn it."

"You bet. Thanks Mister B. You're not a dick like I thought you were. I mean... you're not the jerk I thought you were. I mean... you're okay, Mister B."

"I'm working to not be a dick anymore. Can we leave it at that?"

He smirked, because he and I both knew he would never hear me cuss again, but it offered a strange honesty and vulnerability from both of us.

"Yes, Mister B! I'll try to not be a dick too."

Every time I fail at seeing the complicated person in front of me and I go instead towards my judgment, I am learning a lesson about my own healing. Any judgment I place on another is often a version of the judgment I place on myself. I knew how it felt to be a young child with a story few adults had the patience to discover. I had acted in a similar way and Ian was a mirror for me. Learning to see the compassionate view of Ian was also an invitation to offer this to myself.

All healing begins when we are willing to change the story to a wider view. Our feelings tell us that the hurt we experience is an attack and it feels as if we have been disrespected. Then, we often seek out others to affirm our hurt and build support for our view in the exchange.

This continues to escalate the moment and then it takes on a life of it's own. In mediumship, we are exploring the big picture lessons and stories of a client's beloved in the light. If we understand that hurt is part of every significant relationship, then we can open our hearts to allow the lessons each soul learned through their connection, even if there were a lot of challenges.

We often become more loyal to our hurt than the healing, because we begin to lose hope in the connection. My sadness is woven into your sadness, because I am no longer alone. My journey connects me to you more deeply and certainly, it allows you to connect with me.

Lastly, if we as mediums don't commit to this journey, if we haven't forgiven the people in our story who have harmed us, we can never speak the words of love from a client's loved one who caused pain or harm in a similar way.

Hurting people hurt people.

When we care more about the hurt than the behavior, we will all heal in profound ways. Mediumship cares more about the lessons the hurt inspired, because healing requires the love to win.

Lesson 8 - Mediumship Is Not A Battle Of Good Versus Evil.

"I'm not sure I'm ready for this," a woman paralyzed by fear and shaking in her seat as she chewed on her nails, sits across from me. She is also rocking back and forth. As I observe the turbulent waters of her soul, I begin to wonder the same thing. Maybe, she isn't ready.

I reply, "Don't feel pressured into this. I know your good friend really wanted you to meet with me, but as I often say..." She interrupted me, saying, "It's not that. I met with a medium two years ago, and I'm scared he is still trying to attack me."

In situations like this, I have to be careful. If the client is clearly suffering from severe mental health issues, I have to assess if my work will further a broken reality or provide solace.

I replied, "Tell me what occurred in your first reading. Was it a good experience?"

She began to weep and I was certain that this client was not a good fit. I decided to find a gentle exit out of the session, and then she said, "Brian, the medium said my family is cursed, and I have burned sage everyday to protect my home and my kids. However, I am always afraid I am not doing enough."

I hate conversations like this, because I immediately recognize that a person calling themselves a medium has left this client in a state of emotional peril and offered a ridiculous prescription for the trauma they helped create.

It always seems people doing our work through the lens of fear present some high drama story and then present themselves as the only healer in the world able to wrestle the dark entity their fear has conjured. Seriously????

I proceeded by saying, "I don't believe in that nonsense of curses and I'm so sorry someone doing this work hurt you in that way. That was cruel and ignorant. You deserved better. You are not cursed in any way. Will you trust me to connect with your father?

I feel him with us now."

She jumped out of her chair and froze with fear, "Brian, he's not a good man. Don't let him use you. He can hurt you."

I looked right at her and said, "Love, your dad couldn't harm me and has no desire to harm me. Truthfully, they only come through with messages intended for healing and love. Should we pause and have you reschedule for a time in the future so we can ensure you feel safe and comforted by this experience? There's no rush. You take as much time as you need and reach back to me if you would still like a reading."

She grabbed her bag and held it close to her chest as she walked out of my house. I decided to walk with her to her car and I asked her about her kids and her passions. I realized I needed to ensure she was grounded enough to be able to drive.

Three months later, she appeared back on my schedule, and she greeted me with a completely different energy.

She said, "Brian, I'm so sorry I was such a mess. I was so afraid you would tell me I was cursed and reinforce what I had heard in the past. I'm ready for this. I'm so sorry I wasted an entire session last time."

I replied, "You didn't waste my time in any way, Love. It is an amend from me to you for the harm another person in my work created."

The client was so courageous and inspiring. Her father was a very challenging person in her life. She felt very close to him when she was young, but her parents separated. She would spend summers with him, but he would disappear for days on end and eventually, her mother sought full custody when she was twelve years old. Her father's mental illness deepened and became progressively worse, resulting in no communication when she turned 13.

At the age of 24, she was sent a box in the mail containing a letter with pictures capturing a grisly murder scene. The father wrote her a letter, asking her to come back into his life, so the demon would stop controlling him. She immediately went to the local police and turned in the box and asked for protection until her father was in custody. She had known her father was the one who had murdered her grandparents and her aunt who lived with them, but she had no proof. It took over a month, and they finally found him in the very motel she stayed with him in Reno, Nevada when she was a child.

In the reading, her father shared memories of the younger years when she was lifted on his feet as they played airplane and she learned to dance in his arms. This daughter loved her father, but she couldn't square that against the horrific violence. She never went to visit him in prison, and she never wrote back to his many letters while he was incarcerated.

He died of a heart attack after being incarcerated for over twenty years for murdering his mother, father, and sister.

The father wanted her to know how proud he was of her for getting the police involved and getting him in an environment where he couldn't hurt anyone else. He was a complicated father to a very traumatized daughter. He wasn't a scary soul or frightening in any way. He was a father trying to honor the lessons his daughter was forced to learn in the wake of his mental illness. He wanted her to know he was heartbroken at the pain he created for another, and he kept showing me the pebble in the pond spreading out in ways he never imagined. He spoke of how violence never just hits a target. Rather, it spreads out and disrupts the lives of so many people beyond the victim. He spoke of how he didn't realize how bad things had become, how his drinking combined with a lack of proper medication created a reality that made him feel powerless against the inner voices of fear and terror. He was a desperate person and the help and love he needed never rescued him in his moment of need.

She left my office and reached out with her husband a year later when his mother passed. She even came to visit after her dog died for a reading. It's been eight years since that first connection, and I can only say that the lesson I was offered through her experience is that we are only messengers of love, hope, and healing.

If we feel anything that inspires fear and drama, it is likely not of Spirit. It is likely about our own unaddressed grief and trauma that we are projecting onto our client. "The Botanica Spiritual Center on Federal Boulevard" (name changed to protect the guilty) where she got her multiple readings took over eight thousand dollars from her to abolish this stupid curse crap, and she dutifully paid it.

She believed the medium, because they had some evidence that convinced her. She was also vulnerable in a way most clients are not, because of the trauma this relationship carried throughout her life. The medium even did an exorcism on her and her son. What did that freak show look like? She told this woman that her son had the residue of his grandfather's evil in his aura.

If someone says you or anyone you know has an evil gremlin or demon in your aura, please exit their office immediately. They are not offering you anything other than their fear. They are not mediums; they are traitors of the unconditional love and grace that grounds every interaction in this work.

If you are this person charging people for the darkness and fear you have not healed, please ask for help. Our number one ethical guideline should be to leave a person better than we found them, or at the very least, to do no harm. This intention requires a great deal of consideration from scheduling, pricing, how the reading occurs, and the follow-up we offer when a more serious issue, such as suicide, enters the reading. I'm hoping we as a mediumship community can come together and define our ethical practices that would never be meant to limit our work but simply to provide us a common vernacular to grow towards the very best potential in all of our interactions.

When we sell fear to the world and we get paid to do so, we are also imprisoned by it.

That father was present for a healing and to offer a love he'd always wished to give his one and only child. It was a miracle and a healing of two hearts. The world never honored the heavy burden of his mental illness and the consequence of that was dire and dramatic. However, his lesson is one I honor today. His soul matters to me, and I was grateful to be a witness to the lessons he learned in that darkness. He is a child of God in the same way that all of us are. He is no less deserving of grace than anyone else.

Sadly, the addiction to feeling authority over another can be intoxicating enough that some will never heal this story, because the payoff is worth it for them.

When evidence meets an intention for love and healing, anything is possible. I am not the authority on all issues in mediumship, but I do hope we can ensure that the most vulnerable issues that come into the room offer a hope that will transcend the greatest fears.

This is why we need one another. As we open our hearts to this work, our own fears will spread across all of our work without any negative intent. Having a colleague or mentor to process your fears can ensure you avoid creating narratives that impact your work in the long-term.

Our shared journey can provide a different perspective that ensures Love and Hope lead the way.

Lesson 9 - Mediumship Is A Reminder That We Are All One.

There is no better setting to learn about one-ness than a waiting room at an emergency veterinarian's office.

I was sitting in a waiting room at the Aspen Veterinarian Hospital in Aspen Park, Colorado, as many people patiently waited for the best vet in the world named Doc to call our pet's name. He was a mystical healer that operated in a completely different approach than any other vet I have met. Our dog Miss Ace, an older and wiser gal of twelve-years old, had hip issues and was struggling to hold her urine in the mornings. So, we were back to get her aqua-puncture as he called it which had transformed her hips and restored her ability to retain her urine. She had become a new dog once again.

It was the time of early autumn when the tips of the highest leaves on the aspen groves were just turning yellow, even though the temperature during the day was warm enough to wear shorts. As I sat down in the lobby chairs with National Geographic magazines piled up from many decades inviting me to go on a five-minute daydream to Borneo, my big dog Murphy, a yellow lab rescue, leaned against me with his big blue eyes hoping for a treat to appear because he had been doing such a good job of sitting quietly. He stared and stared as if he was part Vulcan and his mind-meld would soon result in a reward. Instead, I patted Murphy on the head and pulled Miss Ace closer to me on my other side. Murphy then tried the same technique on the room, and it still failed. He then made a frustrated, "Ummmfff," sound as he finally gave into gravity and waited on his back for any person to notice he needed a belly rub stat.

Then, a woman with long grey hair and those weird glasses that go dark when the light is in a room entered the hospital with her little dog making a wheezing sound wrapped in a blanket held to her chest.

Her thick turquoise frames gripped the last bit of the cliff her nose allowed and I could see that she had been crying as the darker lenses faded to clear. She fidgeted with her purse and finally let it drop on the floor as she held her little dog with a pushed-in black face like a standard pug. You could see the blotches of yellow mucus collecting at his nostrils and many bubbles growing and contracting with every labored breath. She wiped them furiously away and then lifted him up to adjust him against her chest as his face rested on her shoulder in the same way a parent would prepare to burp their baby.

His breathing quieted, but the ragged sound of a metallic wash-board being scraped with a nickel occurred with every exhaled breath. I had never heard a sound like that from an animal and I have never heard that ragged pitch again.

She made cooing sounds and whispered, “Baby, Momma’s here. Momma’s here. It’s going to be okay soon, Baby.” She tapped him on the back gently and he coughed and coughed until he passed out against her chest. I wasn’t sure if I should interrupt, so I just tried to look at my shoes and try to assess why my laces always miss the second to last crossover pattern. I always missed the same row near the top for some reason, but it became a much-needed distraction. I’m always amazed at the inane life rafts of thought that appear for me when I need to appear deep in thought.
She interrupted my shoe lace analysis, saying, “You have two big dogs? Don’t you?,” she asked me.
I replied, “Yes, they certainly are. They eat us out of house and home.”

“Will you do me a favor? Enjoy every minute with them, every single minute. Will you promise me that?”

I nodded and I went back to evaluating my shoes again. The intensity of her eyes and the message left me feeling confused and even admonished. I knew that wasn’t what she intended, but vet offices were scary for me. The expensive bills we didn’t always know we could pay and the fears every one of us carry as we bring our companions to be healed one more time can be too vulnerable and intense at times.

I looked over at her and asked, "What's your pug's name?"

"He was my son's dog before he left for college, but now he's all mine. My husband died three years ago from a sudden heart attack, and he is all that is left in our home. My home."
I replied, "He's adorable. Is he struggling with a cold?"

She looked down at her shoes now, but her laces looked flawless. It was literally a perfect brown bow on her brown Bass outdoor shoes with a green rubber lining at the bottom perfect for a bit of slush and snow.

After a time, she replied, "What is wrong with me? His name is Buddy. Buddy is a good boy. He really is a good boy. I can't believe I ever complained about him. You know? Why did I get so upset about him pooping in the house before? It's all so stupid now. Do you know what I mean?"

You can always tell when you are with someone who is alone too much, because they initiate conversation in fits and starts like an old lawnmower motor that hasn't been started in a long time. But, after a bit of time, they find a gentler pace to lob words back and forth. They often reveal too much initially and then rebuild their vulnerability brick by brick as they assess the reaction of the person across from them. However, she was not getting clearer; she was unzipping as her straight-line face became squiggly.

She likely thought, *What the hell is wrong with this weird man staring at his shoes obsessively?*

I replied after a long pause, because I wasn't sure if her question was rhetorical. Then, she stared at me like I was an idiot, so I finally replied in the most eloquent and powerful way I could muster.

I replied, "Yup."

She got the full-on "Yup!" from me that morning, as my introvert and kinda grouchy part of me pulled a fast one on me. That's all that emerged from my mouth, and I desperately hoped for one of our names to be called as soon as possible. I tried being nice, but her level of crazy was too much. I also get this weird southern accent that joins moments like this, which is weird because I'm not from the South and I've barely visited the South.

After the longest five minutes in the world, the front desk person, Karen, came out and guided her back. Karen's scrubs changed seemingly each time, and today, she was covered in pink scrubs with purple pigs on roller skates covering every square inch. Her smile immediately disarmed the most frightened creature as they walked through these doors, which was more often than not the human creature in need of her comforting. Karen came and sat next to me and said, "Brian, we're running a bit late, Jane is saying goodbye to her little guy today. He's a 12-year old pug, which is a miracle. They normally live until the age of 10 due to poor breeding, but she will need some time with Doc. She's been through hell lately. Her husband died after forty years of marriage."

I knew I had failed. The intensity of that moment and her desperation to connect resulted in me closing off to another in need. I knew I had fucked up royally, and I also knew any intervention at this point would only result in making it worse. I would forever be the jerk in the waiting room that stared at his shoes on the day her dog died and said "Yup" with a freaking odd as hell Southern accent as if I was burping up a spirit from a past life who couldn't wait to spread his profound wisdom from his previous lifetime by saying "Yup!" in the most perfectly inappropriate and obnoxious moment possible. Yup! (said with a southern accent)

Let's blame it on a past life.

* * *

It was ten months later that my day to visit that office came. We had said goodbye to Miss Ace by having a hospice vet come to the house, and I had been grieving for four months. Then, Murphy, our rescue yellow lab had stopped eating and couldn't stand on his hind legs. Murphy's large blue eyes told me it needed to happen soon, so I couldn't wait for John to get home from his after-school meetings. I will never forget the entire drive to the vet hospital being filled with Murphy's loud panting and haggard breaths.

When I arrived, Karen greeted me and hugged me. Karen had her dinosaur scrubs that were eating ice cream cones piled so high with scoops they leaned precariously as the large tongues reached out to catch the dripping scoops certain to fall perfectly in their mouths. She went with me to the car with one other person, and Karen said, "Brian, to make him feel safe, why don't you take the side closest to his head so he can see that you're with him?" We carried Murphy out of the car on a blanket. He was a big dog, and it took a lot of effort. They opened the side door into the office and we placed him on the floor.

Karen gazed so kindly at him as she leaned over to hug and kiss him. "Now Murphy, you make sure you meet up with my Sasha and Saski. They'll love having a new friend." Karen then looked right at me, saying, "Those are my hamsters, and they were with me for many years. They're just small dogs basically." I imagined Murphy immediately trying to make them an appetizer, but I smiled politely.

Karen rushed back to her front office to manage the flurry of files and people awaiting her greeting. But, the other person stayed next to me. "Murphy's been a good boy for you all these years, hasn't he?" I looked up, and I saw the turquoise glasses. It was Jane. I had remembered her name. "Yes, he really has. I know it's his time."
Jane placed her arm around me and said, "I had to say goodbye to my little guy, and I thought it would kill me. But, I started work-

ing here a couple months ago and now I volunteer here twice a week. It's so hard to say goodbye to these sweet souls. They teach us to love, don't they? But, then we return the love by knowing when it's time."

I started crying. She held me and gently made circles behind Murphy's ears in the perfect spot he had always loved. Doc came in and just looked at me with his large eyes and gave me the nod of approval, letting me know I had done the right thing. The needle with the bright pink fluid emerged and Doc guided Murphy perfectly as I felt Murphy's head become heavier and heavier in my lap as I stroked the hair on his neck. Jane continued to make gentle circles and pulled me closer as he began to fade.

Jane then said, "Would you like to have Murphy keep his blanket or do you want to take it with you?"

"I'd like to leave it with Murphy." I then moved away from the scene, and my last memory of seeing Murphy was watching her fold him up in his blanket. That dark red and green plaid blanket wrapped perfectly around his body. You could only see the tips of his ears and the top of his head. It was so beautiful and honoring of him.

Jane then spoke soft words of comfort and guided me to my car with her kind eyes and gentle wisdom. As we exited, she said, "You were the perfect companion to Murphy. You really showed your love in the hardest of moments today. Always know that."

I said, "Thank you."

Jane replied, "It was my honor. I want to be the love my Buddy offered me. He saved my life when my husband died. I'm sure your Murphy did the same. It seems the perfect way to return that love."

I replied once again with, "Yup." God, I'm an idiot! I'm not even kidding.

Jane then said, "You seem okay to drive. Just know it was really nice meeting you today. Though I wish it had been under better circumstances. We will light our candle of remembrance for Murphy today and let everyone know a special dog got his wings today."

Jane watched as I drove away, waving to me with tears in her eyes. She didn't remember me, but I could never ever forget her. Jane used all of the words I didn't have for moments like this. Jane had been my teacher from the moment I met her.

Grief is a pair of glasses that always shows me what is important and what really matters. Mediumship is that reminder for me. This work offers me the chance to repay the love that every soul in Spirit has offered me. Jane was teaching me about the wisdom of grief and how love is inexorably sewn into the fabric of that lesson. Jane knew how to hold the space for me as I honored the final act of love required of any person who loves furry spirits.

Mediumship honors this connection and reminds me every day that the soul of you is grieving with the soul of me. We are in the river of grief together, and sometimes my tears are the rapids and other times, yours are. But, we can trust that this flowing river offers an eroding of the anger and the pessimism and the resentment and the hurt and the fears that keep me from seeing the soul in you touching the soul in me.

Jane and her turquoise glasses taught me how to see this calling through different eyes. Through her magical glasses, she knew we were all one in that moment.

Yup!

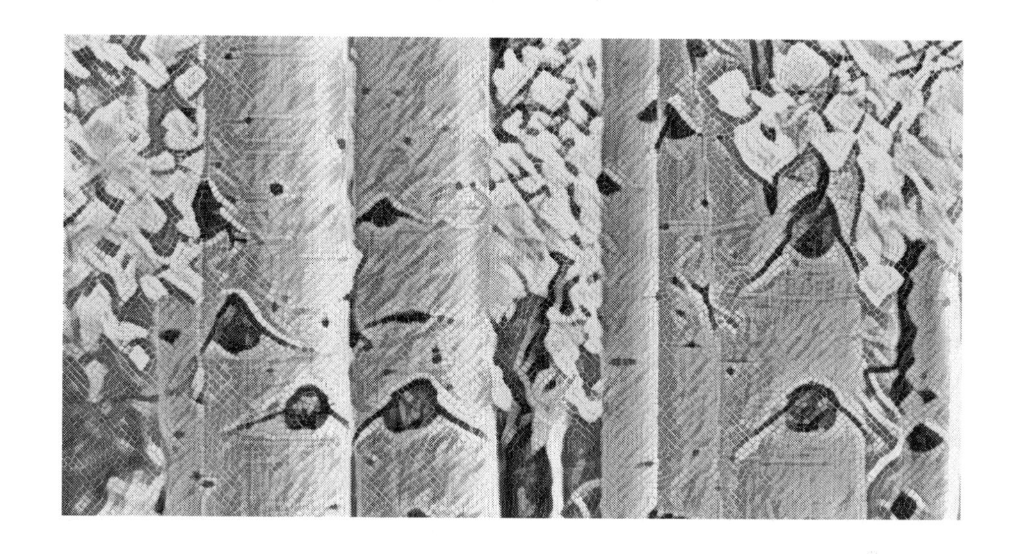

Lesson 10 - Mediumship, In The Highest Form, Can Be An Instrument For Social Justice.

Part 1: My Lessons Through the Window of the Oppressed

As I exited the elevator on the 4th floor of my college dorm, I saw a sign that read,

HOW DID BRIAN GET A HOLE IN HIS BOXERS?
I WONDER... HE'S A FAG-GOT!

There was, weirdly, a butter knife lodged in my very plaid boxers with a hole that was torn through them. I was a freshman attending The Catholic University of America in Washington DC, and I had only told one fellow classmate about being gay. I was in a state of shock for obvious reasons. First, I had never experienced such a public shaming for being gay. Second, I couldn't figure out why they placed a dash in the word faggot. I was left in complete dismay and wondering what did the fag got?

I stuffed everything I could into my green duffel bags and left behind all of my bedding and many of my books, because I was afraid for my two roommates to return. After all, those boxers were mine on that bulletin board. In a moment of a shocking attack, the emotion pulls far back, and a focused mind steps forward. I still don't remember leaving the dorm or packing up my stuff. I just know I carried everything I could, and I remember sitting on the concrete bench at the Metro stop in Brookland, not sure which direction to choose.

My college experience died at Catholic University in a moment, and I was faced with homelessness. Friends around the city gave me a place to sleep, and I would still sneak onto campus for classes. I can't explain why.

The brain doesn't work when things like this occur, so I knew I was supposed to attend school. I raced two times to the Metro with three guys chasing me and threatening to kill me if they saw me on campus again. I'd met with the campus student services office, only to be told that being banished in this way was a natural consequence for the choices I had made. They wouldn't refund a penny for the lodging or the meal plan I couldn't access, so I worked at a pizza place. I was forced to go there on days off to eat. I was couch surfing and eating a lot of pizza.

Being in such a vulnerable position and needing to rely on the kindness of strangers and the not so kind strangers, where nothing was ever free, changed me. I was left in a completely vulnerable position, and I struggled to accept my new reality as parts of my dignity were left in dark hallways and bathrooms across the city. The drugs and the dancing at the gay clubs until 4 AM every weekend became my church.

There were many times during my experience of "coming-out" when I considered suicide. When you believe no one can understand the world you see through the lens of your experience, you begin to no longer feel a part of this world. When hopelessness meets isolation, any person will likely be at risk of suicide.

As a gay person and a member of the LGBTQ community, we are composed of a true constellation of individuals who all have one thing in common regardless of our unique differences – we were all rejected by society for simply being who we were born to be. My story is not unique in any way, and many of my sisters and brothers carry far more painful memories than me. In truth, if we honor that discrimination is a force of hatred and often misplaced self-righteousness, the shame we inflict on a person who is not yet secure with who they are can even create the conditions for suicide.

Our judgment of others that we have not sought to understand or value has real consequences.

Bigotry allows us to not be concerned with the heartfelt needs of another soul, because these belief systems construct language that allows us to see subgroups of people as an “other”. The delineating attribute, an immutable quality of their personhood, is used as a way to separate them from the majority culture.

Mediums do not have the luxury of bigotry, because every soul that comes through us to offer words of hope and healing requires us to vibrate with the very heart of their lessons. Our small-ness will prevent us from accepting the truth of their experience, and we will then be a communicator for the oppression rather than the healing. The way to heal our biases is to notice and name our biases and to engage in a rigorous appraisal of how privilege may impact our awareness in honoring the complexity of a soul.

I promise you that each and every one of us will make mistakes in this complicated arena, but that doesn't give us permission to not do our own work on this. If you are willing to consider the places in your life where you have unearned privileges and also honor the arenas where you may experience some form of discrimination, you will invite a powerful connection to Spirit.

* * *

Part 2: My Lessons Through the Windows of Privilege

Let me invite you into a reading I experienced in a workshop I took one time. It was on the third morning, and we were paired up with a student we hadn't yet worked with. It was a workshop focused on demonstrations, but the teacher often used the mornings to enhance our individual readings, which she often said were the key to being a powerful demonstrating medium.

"I'm Lauren! Nice meeting you. How fun to read a man! Before we start, you need to promise me that you will not connect with my dad. He's been popping through all weekend, and I'm not interested in hearing from that freak. Actually, can we pretend you're number 2? I want to go first!," she said to me.

Lauren stood roughly five foot, ten inches, and she had long platinum blonde hair that had zero movement. She was in her early thirties, because she had expressed that since her thirtieth birthday, she had no clue what color to use for her hair. I heard her joke when she spoke loudly earlier in the day, "Brunettes can be blondes, but we're easy to spot. We're the smart ones who don't need a man to pay our way in the world. I guess we're the smart blondes!" She cackled as the joke escaped her lips.

I replied to her question, "You bet. I'm officially number 2". I then placed my hands in my lap and began to fidget. I always get so nervous during readings in a workshop, because I'm aware that my people in Spirit sometimes wear heels and sequin dresses after Labor Day, which really should be a sin.

It's always fun to watch people work with these fun souls to determine relationship and color of eye shadow.

Lauren leaned back and began to make her link. I could feel the air shift and the bubble of light she was creating for us, as my people came closer and closer. She was clearly doing this professionally, because there were zero nerves.
Lauren said, "Brian, I have a woman with me. She's an older lady, likely in her sixties? This makes no sense to me. I'm likely getting the damn spirit from one of my previous readings. I do hate working in groups. My mediumship is so powerful that it spreads across the whole room, do you know what I mean?"

I reply after an awkward pause, saying, "Tell me more about what you are seeing, feeling, or hearing. There's no need to be nervous with me."

Lauren says, "I am certainly not nervous. I do this professionally. I'm a natural medium. I'm just here learning how to work with the mentoring students I have. I've been training with the Arthur Findlay College for many years."

I replied, "Tell me more about the woman with you."

Lauren said, "Okay. Don't rush me. (Pause) I feel a woman is with us, and it's the same damn person. What the hell is going on? (She looks around the room and faces me.) Does this ever happen to you?"

I interrupted the silence, saying, "I get nervous all the time. It's really okay."

Lauren replied, "I'm not nervous as I've already said. It's just that this damn old black bitch is here, and she should leave us the fuck alone. (She looks around again.) There's no black folks here! Maybe, this woman is here for one of the staff. Or, maybe she's a haunted soul that lives in this hotel. You know that happens. I get hired to work all over the world helping with unwanted souls that still feel as if they own the place, you know what I mean?"
"No, I really don't."
She replies, "Are you new at this?"
"Always."

She sits back in her chair and crosses her arms over her chest, saying, "Well, that's a ridiculous answer."
I then softened my face, because I didn't honestly know what was going to come out of her mouth next. I knew who she likely had, but I didn't want to disrespect her again.

I then said, "I meant to say I'm always new in this work. I never feel as if I can claim to be good at this whole thing. It's..."
She then asks matter of fact, "Are you not a natural at all of this? Are you sure you're a medium then? Many people think they are, but they find...."
"I trust my mediumship. I've had too many experiences that have proven it to me, but can we go back a bit?"
"To which part?"
I said in a bitchy tone, "To the reading part?"

She then pulled herself together and did a deep breath. She finally

spoke, saying, "I don't think I can clear out this old bitty I'm sorry to say. It's likely because I didn't get a great breakfast, and you know what they say – Breakfast is the most important meal of the day. Is there any yogurt here?"
I replied, "Lauren, I believe I know this woman."
"Can you just say Yes or No please?! The old black woman with glasses and a polyester skirt and a white blouse?"
I nodded in agreement, afraid to speak at this point.

Lauren continued, saying, "Even on my worst days, I'm really strong. I knew I had someone for you. Why didn't you say something?"
I replied, "Sorry about that."

She leaned forward again with a large grin, and I was sure this was about to kick into gear. I get nerves too, but then, she said, "I know! Was she an old housekeeper or were you one of those rich families with a governess or a nanny?"

I was really angry and hurt, and I replied, "What made you think she was a housekeeper or nanny?"
She replied, "I think my time is up, so let's switch. I can guide you if you need my support."
I said quietly, "You're right."
She asked, "Right about what?"
"Our time is up," I said, as I stood up and left the classroom.

I leaned against the wall in the large lobby of this humongous church hall. I called my friend Kim, and I was more emotional than I expected myself to be. Then, I started to minimize in my head what happened, and I started to diminish my feelings by saying things like, *Don't be so dramatic. She's a student too. We all have an off day.*

My friend Kim said so clearly after I told her the entire story, "Brian you need to tell her how that felt. She likely has no clue what she said, and let's be honest. This is what people of color have to put up with all the time. You get to walk away when many we know cannot."

Here's the part where you can hopefully learn from me. I so wish I could tell you a different ending, but I can't.

I didn't say one thing to her, and she never spoke to me during the rest of the workshop.

Weirdly, we ended up sitting together at a table over lunch at a local restaurant. Our invite came from the same kind man who organizes, to this day, great mediumship workshops and events in the Denver area. Lauren and I barely caught eyes, and we both pretended our interaction had never occurred. She likely thought I was being overly sensitive, and I was afraid to tell her how this felt.

On that final day, I sat in my car and wondered why I never said anything to her. It hurt so much for her to assume Dorothy was my housekeeper or my nanny. Dorothy lived across the street from us when I was a child, and her home became a sanctuary for me. I would visit her every day, and she always offered me lemon drops candies and held me in her lap as she read to me. One day, she surprised me with a cake cooked in the Winnie the Pooh pan she found at a garage sale. I will never forget sitting at her table and eating that yellow cake with chocolate frosting as Dorothy smiled across the table.

Lauren couldn't allow this relationship to be honored through her. If she had paused and worked through her confusion, she would have learned a valuable lesson. She would come to realize that some grandmothers are chosen. Dorothy was a highly educated professor. She taught at universities and became an emeritus at universities for two years at a time after her retirement, even teaching in Europe. I cannot imagine the walls she knocked down and how that experience created a grace and kindness I have seldom experienced in my life. This student would have been transformed by this soul's invitation. But, her story about a woman of color could not allow the truth of Dorothy to be honored.

As I became more aware of my privileges as a white male in our country, I also began to revisit pivotal memories from my childhood to really understand the impact this had on others in my life. In first grade, I remembered my friend Demerius and how his darker skin created a completely different response from our first grade teacher. When Demerius and I acted out, often with me as the catalyst, Demerius was held after school and told to stop being disruptive.
I was told that I wasn't living up to my potential. I remember the constant refrain from the teacher, saying to me and my parents, "Brian has an incredible amount of potential. He just needs to focus and make wiser choices so he isn't influenced by negative peers."

Demerius was told he was a delinquent, and I was told I was gifted and not living up to my potential. The behaviors were the exact same, but the stories regarding the intent and purpose were in no way the same. Many would have had a hard time addressing this as racism, but it was exactly that. I wasn't in any way aware at the time, and I remember believing I was somehow more endowed with natural intelligence because that was the very message placed at my feet every day. Demerius was left out of that hopeful promise for his dreams and his true purpose.

How do we imagine hearing this message every day in the mind of a seven-year old going to influence how he feels about being a student in school? The devastation of racism is that if you are not the one experiencing the oppression, then you are often benefitting from it.

The same first grade teacher placed names on the board and check marks by our names when we were caught talking or off-task. I remember when he received check marks for my talking in class that this was an unfair system.

His eyes changed, and we were no longer friends after fourth grade. How could our friendship overcome that imbalance and the cruelty he faced on a daily basis? He left our Catholic elementary school to attend the local public school, and I don't remember him raising his hand in class even once in fourth grade. His body had been in the chair during fourth grade, but his light and value never returned during his final year at our school.

There are real consequences to racism in all of it's forms, and until we as mediums care more about the profound hurt and long-term pain of being disregarded, we will never be able to truly honor the wisdom and dignity of our sisters and brothers of color. It's not about making assumptions regarding the hurt or only highlighting the challenges people experience. It is about seeing and honoring the internal wisdom and perseverance that some roads in life require.

I offer this as my amend for failing to use the voice I didn't earn to empower my friends of color who had to fight to have their voices acknowledged. This occurred at least eight years ago, and I will never fail Dorothy and Demerius again in this way. The world can be a profoundly unfair and cruel place at times, and I have failed in far more ways than this regarding race. My biases and ignorance spoke loudly when I was younger. I often used racial slurs as a way to push the focus of me being gay onto someone else when I was younger. So, please do not read this and see me as a white savior for people of color. That's not the case either. I am no longer suffering from the disease of white fragility, and I can hear and honor when my courageous friends highlight when I speak from bias or disempower a person sometimes when my intent was to support.

Some might say that I am too concerned with being politically correct. As a medium, I am a vessel for a Spirit to share their story - the memories, the lessons, and the love. If I diminish the authentic experience of a loved one in the light and discount the hurt, the humiliation, the grief, and the trauma of their experience, how can I possibly say I am doing my job? If I cannot celebrate the accomplishments, the pride, the hope, the courage, the resolve, and the resilience required, am I truly honoring their beloved?

I am a student of this lesson and not a teacher. It is a returning of the grace that has been given to me by every person of color I failed to see. It is a returning of the respect that was shared with me by my friends of color that had the courage to tell me the truth about myself. It is a returning of the kindness to know the patience I required of them as they planted seeds of possibility in me, hoping one day, I would awaken.

When someone cares more about your character than your approval, they are a gift to your soul. They believe a better version of you is waiting to be born. They see the possibility of your soul while the world has to deal with the reality of it.

Lastly, the danger in writing something like this is that people will then celebrate the author and see me as some courageous caring soul. I would recommend you re-read this if that is the impression you are carrying. When we finally begin to honor the hurt we have created after failing to do so for many years, casting me as some white hero in the story simply proves my privilege. I was part of the problem for many years of my life, and I am seeking to heal the wounds I created and facilitated in this life.

If you are inspired, join me in doing your own work around this. Join me in honoring that the suffering and hurt generations of people of color have experienced matters, and that you likely contributed to that suffering, either consciously or unconsciously. This topic requires a great deal more time and attention, and there are some incredible teachers in our community doing this work. I am limited by my experiences in this life, so my stories are also only able to explore the perimeter of my world.

So, please consider opening a new door to this possibility of your soul. The teachers that await us are ready. I look forward to learning from them and growing more in this arena of my development.

Mediumship is a process of honoring the story of every Spirit. As we grow in these ways, the story sings, the healing grows, and the soul expands.

Lesson 11 - Your Greatest Teacher In Mediumship Is Always Your Most Challenging Client.

I remember hearing in a workshop one time a fascinating question that I had been struggling with myself at the time.

The student asked, "How do I deal with a difficult client?"

The teacher replied, "There are a lot of different challenges clients can present in our work. Can you be more specific?"

The student continued, "Well, I guess it is the clients that say everything you offer is wrong."
The teacher walked to the center of the classroom and looked at all of us.

She said, "I don't waste time on clients like that. They will sap the energy right out of you. If I offer four to five pieces of evidence, and they won't take any of it. I immediately shut down the reading and recommend they work with another medium."

I couldn't disagree more with this approach. These are my favorite clients, because they will make you great at this work. I don't even care if these clients pay honestly. They are my greatest teachers in the most critical lesson in the practice of mediumship – to trust Spirit and to not abandon Spirit when you aren't getting the "Yes" you are hoping to hear.

Besides, if we are only effective with clients who believe in what we do, how many loved ones in the light are we unwilling to witness? How many suffering people are we missing the opportunity to serve through the miraculous experience mediumship offers?

When the grouchy ones arrive, I'm often saying to Spirit,

Thanks for the grouchy ones! I know they need my time just as much, if not more, than other clients. I trust their loved ones to connect with their heart. I surrender the rest.

* * *

The Grieving Widow

I will never forget the client who changed my focus in this work. The client was holding tightly to her grief and she was doing everything she could to maintain a careful speech pattern to not give away any impressions. As we started the phone call, she said, "I don't really know why I'm even doing this. I don't believe in what you do. My friend told me to call, so I just thought I'd see what tricks you played on her. I won't be as easy to manipulate."

I paused, and I felt the nerves rise in me, and I immediately wanted to cancel the reading. I immediately replied with, "Don't you worry. I don't believe in this either. So, let's just see what happens, and maybe we will both be surprised." Her defenses didn't change one bit.

I took some deep breaths and continued with the reading. She was basically distant and non-responsive most of the reading. There were times I would check the information I knew in my gut was accurate, and she would say things like, "not quite" or "not really" or "that's true for any person." Then, her husband who had recently died came into the circle of light. His soft face, drooping eyes, and cowboy hat filled my eyes, and he was clearly a complicated soul who was mostly introverted in life. This reading turned out to be ninety-minutes long, and she was completely dissatisfied.

So, I didn't charge and I suggested she reach out in a couple of months if she wanted to try again. I often suggest meeting in person the next time, because the human-to-human connection can sometimes create a stronger sense of trust.

However, a week later, I got a message from her asking me to call. She had listened to the recording multiple times, and she said, "Brian, you knew things about my husband I've never told another soul. You even described our couch and the large television where we always watched movies. I was so distraught and I assumed this was all a manipulation. Now, I know he is with me. I felt him, but now I really trust it.." Then, she started to weep on the other side of the phone openly with me, and I simply listened. I was shocked that it was the couch with recliners on both ends and their DVD collection that was the clincher for her, but this is why I trust the loved one in the light.

She was also protecting her grief, because vulnerability must be earned with a suffering person. They spend so much time pretending to the world that they are okay, even if they aren't. Our society often demands this from grieving people. Dropping your defenses with a stranger on the phone the first time is asking a lot from a client. Certain clients need more time to process the experience and to revisit the reading. I'm actually no different than her when I'm hurting.

The message of her husband's eternal love made it to her ears through the recording. I was no longer a variable, and the recording was hers to explore at her leisure. Recording the readings for your clients has become easier than ever, and it provides an artifact of that moment many clients will revisit. Grief will always remind us to feel the connection we desperately miss, because our love continues long after death.

This client has attended almost every local event I have done and she reaches out on a regular basis for us to get a meal or do a reading. She has become a dear friend.

This grieving widow was trying to find a reason to live again. If I had responded to her behavior with the advice I had been given, I would have missed out on that ninety-minute reading where I surrendered to her loved ones and she would have missed the miracle of trusting that her loving husband is still present in her life.

Mediumship is a form of service. When we are willing to place our needs for validation and approval in the background, our work takes on new possibilities. We can create a link with a person's loved ones, even if they are not in the right frame of mind to receive the information. Grief takes on many forms, and sometimes, we must be careful to not over-react to a person's fear and deep-seated grief.

I've never come across a client setting up a reading to just prove that you suck at your job. Any person who contacts you, whether they know it or not, are hoping for a miracle. I always trust Spirit to provide that miracle. When we trust Spirit to this degree, there is a gift of peace that permeates the work and a joy that accompanies every connection.

* * *

It is enough to be washed in the love and feel the song of hope and healing be played with the very strings of your heart.

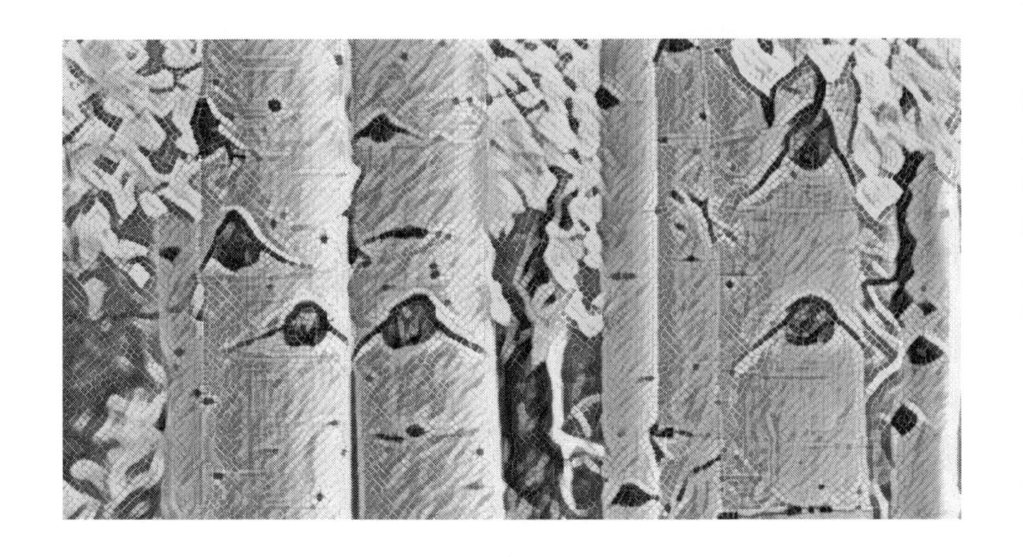

Lesson 12 - Mediumship Is A Call To Befriend Death.

This lesson took many years to write. I would start the story, but it would feel too sharp and have too many edges. This is the moment when I met Death in the most personal way, and I was left with a lesson in loss that still unfolds and deepens today. This meeting with Death is the moment when my calling to mediumship became set against my soul.

This is the lesson I wish that I never had to write, but I am not alone in this lesson. Any person who has loved will understand the dimensions of this grief and the lessons Death offers when we begin to see her as the kind friend she truly is.

* * *

Marc with a C

"Two weeks?!? There's no fucking way. Are you serious right now? Why does it take so damn long?," I screamed at the at-risk counselor.

He leaned forward and placed his hand on my leg in an oddly comforting way. His blue eyes looked at mine and then took a big sighing kinda breath, where he was unconsciously hoping he could get me to relax too. It worked.

The at-risk counselor said, "I remember when I first got tested. It felt like two weeks of revisiting every single sexual episode I had ever experienced. I felt as if Sister Mary Margaret from my Catholic School was tsk-tsk-ing me as she looked over her spectacles with her certain expression that told me that she knew. She was the one person I couldn't deceive."

"Look, Mr. At-Risk Counselor! I'm sure your childhood was rough, but can you please tell me if there is any way that I can get these results sooner? I can't wait for two weeks."

"Matt. My name is Matt. I'm new here, so my teammate gave me this badge they have volunteers wear."

I replied swiftly to avoid hearing any more of his droning memoir, "At-risk counselor? You're seriously kidding with that. Am I really at risk?"
"We all are. But, you clearly know that. Otherwise, you wouldn't be here." I hate when people that wear badges are actually good at that thing their badge says they are good at.
Matt continued, "I bet you now have a reason for living. So, now, you're here to find out if you are going to complete that thing or love that person you didn't have in your life six months ago."
I replied with a nod. He was kinda right.
"Brian, when I found out I was HIV positive, I thought I was dying. I don't remember the Metro ride home or even if I ate dinner that night. But, I remember thinking that every decision matters now."
I replied, "Okay Matt the At-Risk Counselor, I'll get tested."

Matt smiled and his big teeth revealed themselves, and I noticed the edges of a tattoo crossing his chest that looked like a wing of a bird ending at the base of his neck. I was strangely attracted to him and the intensity of it surprised me, but I could tell that this had occurred for him many times. He leaned back in his chair in a perfect dance to let me know that this was not going to be that kind of HIV testing experience.

As I stood up to go and felt the handle of the door in my grip, I turned back to him and said, "How'd you do it? How'd you accept this whole fucking thing?"
He crossed his arms across his chest, and he said, "I don't have an answer for that. It's not one thing to accept; it's a million. Every day, I see or I feel or I notice how HIV has changed me. Some days, I'm pissed off, and other days, I'm more grateful than I have ever been."
"Grateful?," I replied. "I can't even imagine that."
Matt laughed and his arms unfolded as he crossed his legs, "Brian, you have two weeks in front of you to become the person who can accept whatever result you are handed in two weeks. Two weeks

is a lot longer time than you may imagine. But, you have two weeks to become the person who can live with either conclusion. Does that make sense?"
I replied, "Not really."

Matt stood up and walked over to me, saying, "Brian, are you a spiritual kinda person?"
"I was brought up Catholic, so let's just say..."
Matt interrupted me, saying, "You were going to be funny again. Look at me for a second. You have two weeks to get a God that is strong enough and powerful enough for you to accept whatever answer awaits you. Until then, don't come back, because the results won't matter. You're already dying."

Then, he held me. I didn't know where to place my hands, so they dangled there until I finally hugged him back. I was angry with him and also grateful for him. He didn't once ask me about every Twister move I did on the board completely naked that could have exposed me to HIV, and he also didn't demonstrate how to put a condom on a perfectly innocent banana that never did anything to anyone. If I'm honest, I kept revisiting the time my feet were both on green, and my right hand was on blue with my left on red. His name had been Henri with an "I", and no condom entered the picture. It happened once 9 months ago, and he'd told our common friends right after the event. Roughly ten days prior, I'd found out that Henri moved back home because of his HIV advancing to a point where he needed the support of family. My friend Dan told me by phone, and he said, "I thought you deserved to know."

I knew I needed to get tested, and I knew I was positive. One night, after the lights were turned up to the brightest level possible at Track's Nightclub in Washington DC, Henri and I caught one another's eyes. We knew some of the same fellas from Friday afternoons at JR's Bar on 17th Street near Dupont Circle, so we at least knew each other a teeny-weeny bit. It was not a fierce attraction needing to be satisfied. It was honestly more like a shrug and a quiet surrender to a need to be touched winning out for both of us. It wasn't even alcohol-related, because I'd always struggled with an adverse reaction to alcohol. It was just the presence of another and we both signed the same contract as we made our way to his fifth-floor apartment in the Navy Yard, notarizing it by accepting his full-mouthed kisses in the cab.

His kiss was desperate and confusing as he came in strong and withdrew with bizarre and random laughs which felt at my expense in some way. I kept wondering if there was an invisible third person he was performing for, but this never felt right. My body screamed to abandon ship, but the cab fare to a different neighborhood as the sun was rising over the city made this feel inevitable. After all, the Metro didn't start running until 8 AM on Sundays, so the stairs to his apartment caused me to think about the descending feeling of doom after sex. Is this the part when I should have been humming, "I Cain't Say No" from Oklahoma? (Are you really surprised a musical reference made it into this piece?)

Henri said, "I can't believe we're going to have sex. You're mostly a tease, you know? At least, that's what the word on the street is."
I replied, "Yeah, I can see that. Some people use sex to feel alive, and some use it to forget."
Henri looked curious as he said, "Which one are you?"
I smiled and kissed him again, holding his thin frame close to me. I said, "Does it really matter?"
Sex was confusing, because my body had been used against me by a man with a collar and a man with no collar. One man showed me how love can shine a light against the rooms of your soul and restore you. That man was gone, so tonight was a night for forgetting.

So, when the forms asked in multiple ways if I had been exposed to the HIV virus, I replied NO. My shame spoke louder than the truth, and I had a plan to say I was just curious about how the testing process worked, but Matt never asked me. I wanted to blame Henri, but I allowed it. I said, "Do what feels good for you," because I didn't matter yet. He never said a word about HIV, so we were both silent about the truth in that moment.

Two weeks ahead of me and a daunting as hell task. How does a failed Catholic who is openly gay attending the Catholic University of America in Washington DC get a God that will help me walk confidently into that testing center at the Whitman Walker Clinic and embrace whatever answer is waiting for me?

Then, I saw his face. His blue eyes framed by a halo of short brown curly locks staring at me with his wise grin. He was smiling as he chewed on the toothpick that seemed to last forever. His light blue sweatshirt with his old alma mater in sewn-on stencil letters spelled DUKE. The "K" hung precariously on one corner waiting for a rough breeze or a dryer to accomplish the task. He returned to me as I walked the steps briskly to get back on the Metro at Dupont Circle to catch the red line train to Brookland/CUA Stop where a couch awaited me at my friend Richard's apartment. I was no longer able to be in the dorms after being outed by a woman I'll call Super-Bitch. She used to be Super-Satanic-Bitch. That's called growth, people.

Marc was with me that evening. I was certain of it and yet completely skeptical. Marc was gone. His father's letter told the tale. He was dead. Six feet under. Isn't that the way we describe what happens to faggots who never sought forgiveness for their perverse lifestyle? I wasn't always the activist type who dropped the gay bomb within my first breath. I used to be reserved about such things, because I was certain something was wrong with me. God dropped the ball at some point. In the assembly line of souls, someone dropped a pink triangle in my soul, and the quality control team was on break. It was really their fault, but in two weeks, I would know if my life was walking a very different timeline.

When I first saw Marc, it wasn't a West Side Story where I was ready to climb fire escapes and abandon my family heritage for love. In that moment at Paradise Garage under the old concrete viaducts in Denver, a hot nightclub was pumping out music. Jimmy Sommerville was raising his voice to a soprano line asking for the "Smalltown Boy" that was gay to have a chance at love. Marc was in my vision as this song faded, as Madonna's "Erotica" chimed in.

Marc was a Greek God! I'm not exaggerating. I saw the biceps of his arms contract and release as he lifted drinks up and down from the bar, laughing with the bartender. Then, I walked over to order any drink possible with my new fake ID saying I was 23 at the ripe age of 17.

"Could I get a single malt scotch?," I said, because I knew my dad's drink of choice would make me look cool. (Before you start judging, I was turning up the sexiness to the highest volume it would go. Dungeons and Dragons had not prepared me for this moment. Is it a sixteen-sided die at this moment and how many hit points do I need?)
He stood there and adjusted himself to my presence. My sexy vibe threw him off.
"What's the weather like?," I asked. This isn't even me joking. Yup. That was the best I had to offer.
"Uh... have you been outside today?"
"Well, yes. It's nice but chilly outside. You know what I mean?"
He replied with that smile that immediately disarmed me as he said, "I wouldn't recommend becoming a meteorologist, but I think I know exactly what you mean. Tell me your name and shake my hand while keeping eye contact."
"My name is Brian. I'm nice to meet you. I mean... it's nice to meet you." Oh Fuck! Okay, maybe I am Maria in this story. Damn it.
"Brian, eh? I'm Marc."

A bizarre pause filled the space, and Frank the Bartender interrupted our love story by asking, "Hey Young Man! When were you born?"

"November 1st, 1971." Damn. As it escaped my lips, I realized my name on the fake ID that clearly said "David Saint Michael" with a different birthdate (Only a Catholic boy would try to use a fake ID with a saint's name).

Frank leaned over and looked at my ID. Then, he grabbed the soda gun and filled up the glass, saying, "Here's the Coke you ordered" as he winked at me to let me know my secret was safe with him.

Marc then looked at me with his very kind blue eyes, saying "Here's where you ask me some questions."
"Oh! Sorry. Umm.... How's it going?"
Marc replied, "It's going great. Keep your eyes on me so I know you're really interested."
"Okey dokey." WTF? I've got no game. None. Less than none!
"Well, I'm not really available to date right now, but use these steps when meeting a new fella. You'll be just fine, and you might run a comb through your hair."
"Thanks. Can I at least know your name?"
Marc replied, "Marc."
"Nice meeting you, Marc."
"Nice meeting you, Brady. You're getting better at this. Good eye contact."
I replied, "Thanks again, Marc. My name is actually Brian."
"Brian? With an "I" or "Y"?"
"With an "I"."
"I dated a Brian a long time ago. He was a jerk."
"Let me break you of the Brian Curse!"

Marc replied, "Enjoy your Coke with no scotch. Enjoy your youth and be safe out there."
He left. I'd destroyed any chance to ever have Tony on my balcony singing musical tunes outside my window. Come to think of it – Tony is a tenor, and Marc was all baritone. That sexy voice, the tufts of brown hair trying to free themselves of the woven cotton undershirt, and his gait made it clear that he was the reincarnation of a dime store cowboy.

I'm dumb about westerns, so I then became completely lost as the film references I had as a 17-year old junior at Regis Jesuit Catholic High School provided no context to capture this moment.

I'd met a Marc, and tonight was not the night. Screw you, Bernstein! Where's the song for this moment? (Another musical reference!!! Are you keeping count?) There are moments where even I hate musicals.

As luck would have it, I saw him again at a party of a fella named Rob. (By the way, if you're trying to avoid having a gay son, I hope you're noticing a pattern to the names. Duh, people!)
Marc saw me and smiled immediately, like you would if a girl you once dated that you wished had drowned that summer approached you at a party.

"Hey Marc! Do you remember me?"
"Of course, I do. How could I forget? Future meteorologist?"
"That's me. It's Brian."
Marc replied, "Oh, I remember," and then he turned away to stare at a hideous painting of a mountain meadow that suddenly captivated him.
I asked, "Was it with a "I" or a "Y"?"
"Huh?"
"Was your previous Brian an "I" or a "Y"?"
Marc turned around and looked right at me, and then he smiled. This was a real one though. It passed the boundary of social grace into something else. Curiosity?
Then, Marc asked, "It doesn't matter, because that's not what's happening here, Brian with an 'I". Are you of age?"
"It's November 17th. I have been 18 for 17 days. How old are you, wise old man?"
He replied, "28 years old. So, I guess that makes me your elder. But, I don't date children. So, let's get this straight at the beginning. I'm happy to be a friend. That's all."
"You'll be my Mister Miyagi?"

Marc looked puzzled, even though he got that reference. Maybe, Mister Miyagi was too old of a reference.
Marc replied, "I'll be your older friend that will do what I can to prepare you for the crazy world you're about to enter." He then reached out his hand, as if we needed to honor this contract somehow.

I shook his hand in agreement, but I definitely crossed my toes hoping someday that Mister Miyagi would become my Tony, except the stocky brown-haired Greek God with the sweet baritone voice version.

Six months later of working on our friendship and meeting him at the local park where sexy gay guys played volleyball on Saturdays, a tall man named Vincent had his eyes on me and kept touching my butt every time we crossed to the other side of the net. It was the third game, and I was the worst volleyball player they had on the field that day, but Vincent was definitely interested. His bald head gleamed in the sun, and his eyes leered at me through the net. Every time I tried to avoid crossing the net with him, he would always move to get into my lane. As the middle of the third game invited the crossover, Vincent came for me with his 6'2" frame and placed both of his hands on my butt, saying, "I'd love to spike that ass."

Marc lifted the net and walled right up to him. Marc's 5'9" frame met Vincent's gargantuan and unreasonably sweaty body with Marc's arms flexed against the "EARTH DAY" t-shirt Marc had worn out many times over. The t-shirt had the planet with humpback whales swimming in a circle around a peace sign.

Mark yelled loudly, "What the fuck is wrong with you? Get your hands off of him." Marc was bigger in stature than Vincent, and the argument immediately ended as it started. Marc then raised his hand to me, saying, "Come on, Brian. It's time to go." Maybe, this was my West Side Story, and I'm definitely Maria.

As we exited the field to climb into his dark green Volkswagen Jetta with a sunroof, we drove away as Marc broke the silence. "My first Brian was with a Y." I had just become his second.

That night would be our first date. I picked him up exactly at the time he asked, and we went to the movie "Henry – the Portrait of a Serial Killer" at the Mayan Movie Palace (Again, don't judge. It worked. Popcorn plus scary movie equals good times!) right near his home. Halfway through the movie, Marc placed his left hand on my right thigh. He didn't just let it rest there. He grabbed my leg in his and held it gently but with stability. After ten minutes, he whispered into my ear, "You can rest your right hand on mine if it feels right."

The gentle smell of his Fahrenheit cologne with a note of cedar and cinnamon hit my nostrils whenever he would move closer to me in that chair. I have never despised an arm rest more than I did in that moment.

When we were sitting on his couch after a movie I barely remembered, his Saint Bernard named "Lady" stared softly at me panting until she finally lowered herself all the way to the floor with a large sigh. Marc started to move his hands back and forth over his thighs tightening his fingers with each passing stroke. The air became crisp and the taste of saccharin that lives on the tongue after slugging down a diet drink filled my mouth. I felt the words before his mouth opened.
"Brian, I'm HIV positive."

I can't write the rest of what occurred that night. My eighteen years and six months had not prepared me for this moment. Marc was infected. He was sick. He had the plague, and I replayed every interaction I'd ever had with him to ensure no exposure had occurred. My immediate reaction felt wrong, but fear has a cadence that sometimes takes the higher chord, drowning out all of the others.

There was a fermata being held with each passing moment as the waves of his statement landed on shore many times until he broke the trance by saying, "Brian, do you understand how a person gets HIV?"

I didn't. I know many reading this will think of me as an uneducated idiot at that point, but gay sex still felt like drinking under age. It was exciting, and the desperation that gripped me around this attraction to men felt like an addiction. I was trying to finally taste the forbidden fruit. In that desperate note of attraction, the chord of fear and death would rise and rise. Then, the desperation would return.

I replied, "No."

He could tell the light in my eyes had dimmed, and that I was not able to hold this space with him. He walked me to my car and held my door for me. He went to kiss me, and I turned away.
HIV meant death to me, and I knew I would die too. But, I wanted to do whatever I could to hasten that death. The next morning, Marc called me, and his baritone voice filled the speaker.

"Brian, please just listen. I understand if you don't think you can do this. I wouldn't blame you. I really wouldn't, but I need you to be honest with me."
"No Marc. I want to do this. I really do. I'm just not sure how to..."
Marc replied, "It is my job to protect you. I won't allow you to do anything that places you at risk."
"How did you get this?," I asked.
"From the Brian with a Y."

That summer, Marc and I made out and held hands for many weeks. Then, one night, he was wearing that damn sexy Earth Day t-shirt. I knew I was ready. As I removed his t-shirt, his large torso and hairy chest revealed a strong and powerful man.
"Marc, why do you keep this old t-shirt that is barely holding together?"

"Brian, this t-shirt has been with me for a long time. It was given to me by a dear friend when I was first diagnosed with HIV."
"But why this t-shirt? It's just a shirt."
"You see an old tattered shirt, but I see a reminder of how many days I have walked this Earth since the day I knew I was going to die."
Marc picked it back up and held it up. "How do Humpback whales migrate across oceans every year to have their babies?"
"I have no clue."
"Exactly. You see an old shirt, but I see a map."
I replied, "a map?"
"A map doesn't always just tell you where you're going. It tells you how to get back home."

Okay, I get it. He's a bit Mister Miyagi if Mister Miyagi had been hot as hell.

That evening, Marc showed me how a man makes love to another man with no risk whatsoever. One might say we waxed on and then waxed off (terrible joke!). This would be the first time where guilt offered no response. My heart was lighter than it had ever been, and I knew that Marc would never again be Mister Miyagi. He had become something new words had to follow in the wake of this new world he had offered with every one of his kisses. A man could love another, and my world had been tilted onto a completely different axis. I was born again as love songs on the radio seemed to track the undulating pathway of our vulnerability.

Every first love must end. It crescendos in early August, as the afternoon breezes promise the return of winter's song. These songs of the season are carried on the wind, and experience allows us to hear the complexity, depth, and power each song offers. Our ears must change for these songs to cross the river of reason. Love carries a tune against the flat notes of fear and dread.

"Brian, we need to be done," Marc said.
"What do you mean?," I said.
"You're going to college, and I'm...," Marc said.
"We talked about this. Marc, don't...," I pleaded.
"We are done. Things are not.... I have AIDS."
"No!"
"Yes, Brian. I'm officially below 200. I'm moving in with my dad. You must trust me."
I was getting ready to launch my life, and he was accepting the ending of his.
"Marc, come on. We can go through this together."
"Brian, we knew this had an end date. I love you."

The first time he said those words offered an ending.

As that old AT&T light blue phone clicked against the metal cradle offering a ting sound, the phone quieted and then the emptiest note greeted me developed by the cruelest person working at the phone company – the single note letting you know the call had truly ended. That sound awaited a new number to be dialed or it would soon boom at me. I held the phone and tried to will this moment into the past with imagined fantasies of this call having never occurred.

Part of me understood. I didn't fight for him. The song of fear was still playing under the passion and possibility. The two dark Rohrshoch irregular circles on his torso with a purple line around the brown foretold the rest of the story. It is the moment in a score when a conductor warns you that this won't be easy to complete. Even though we love the Pie Jesu in every Requiem, that song only makes sense anchored between the verses of despair and horror.

In 1991, two years later, I would get a call in the fall of my sophomore year, and Marc's voice greeted me in the static.

Marc asked, "Is this the Brian with an I?"
"Yes". That's all I could say.
"Brian, I don't have a lot of time, but you need you to know something."
His energy swam across the phone lines and he was in front of me with his blue eyes. He was right there, and any static temporarily vanished.
"Of course, Marc. I'm listening."
"Brian, I'm at the hospital in San Francisco. My dad is with me."
"You made it to California to be with your dad? That's great!" I ignored the word "hospital" completely. It had a different note, and my brain was tossing that one around waiting for it to land.
"Brian, I don't have long now."
"Marc, I...."
Marc responded, "Brian, I'm sorry to drop this bomb. I need you to know I loved you. I mean, "I love you". I always have. My dad will be reaching out to you after..."
I heard his tears fill the phone, and his dad grabbed the phone. "Marc needs to go. He needs his rest."

That was all. Three days later, his father left a voice message letting me know that his son Marc, my Marc, the only Marc with a "C" I've ever known, had died that morning.

At that time, Death was final and unforgiving. I had met Death for the first time, and that bitch and I were not yet on speaking terms.

The package arrived from his dad two weeks later. I have no memory of providing him my address at 609 A Street, SE in Washington DC. The father used all capital letters in his writing just as Marc did. I do this now myself ever since Marc died. As I write this, I never made this connection until this very moment. I placed that package into my green duffel bag from Land's End that was used to move me to DC when I first left home. I wrapped the bag tightly after I zipped up the contents. I knew it was a VHS Copy of the Karate Kid, but I just couldn't bring myself to open it. This is a package you only get to open once.

Two months later, I went to the Whitman Walker Clinic to get tested. I was out walking and walking trying to find a God large enough for me to return to get those results. It was never the touch of Marc that had worried me. Rather, it was the cold sexual experiences trying to forget that had led me to that terror. When you think you are a piece of crap, there is nothing to protect.

As I sought and sought by praying in churches, meditating to Buddha, taking long walks, and writing a prayer of hope, I was left with no God and one day to return for my results at 5:30 PM at the Whitman Walker Clinic. My roommate Jim would meet me there because he was serving in the food bank that night.

That night, I felt very strongly that I needed to open the box that sat in the bottom of a closet wrapped in a duffel bag. There was a small envelope with my name written across - BRIAN WITH AN I. I thought it was a joke from Marc, but it turned out to be a letter from his dad. It was on basic white stationary and his father thanked me for loving his son. The idea of a father thanking me for loving his son was hard to imagine, and yet, this letter in three sentences offered the gentle words of a father from the heart of his gentle son.

As I opened the box, I saw a shoebox with the word BASS written on it. It was so light and made not a sound. As I opened it, the white perfectly folded t-shirt I had begged him to throw out emerged. The circle of blues and purples ran together.

Then, the peace symbol emerged. I saw it fully for the first time. Peace. Marc was at peace. It had truly been a map.
I felt a peace beyond words wash over me as I held that t-shirt close to me. The smell of his Fahrenheit cologne greeted me, and I knew that he was with me. I couldn't believe in a God, but I believed in him.

The results awaiting me were no longer about an ending or a beginning. He was home, and I was home, even if this awareness lasted a nanosecond.

The test began many years ago, and this was another lesson to be tested many times in the future, although results now come in 15 minutes. It is an annual ritual where I ensure my God is big enough to accept the arrow on the map.

I now know the destination is always peace.

The destination was at the center of his shirt where the peace symbol lived. Peace is always the center of every maze. The soft belly, the acceptance, the gratitude, the whispers of those beyond us, the tears, the prayers, and the open arms to every moment and finally, the deep breath.

Death is always holding hands with Love.

EPILOGUE - THE PORCHLIGHT

"You really must buy. You aren't getting what a great deal this timeshare is!" Lola, the stern, platinum blonde realtor blinked her puppy-dog eyes at us as she made her final pitch, trying to get us to buy a timeshare. The small cinnamon rolls I was inhaling tasted bitter. She ran her manicured hand through her hair and smiled, baring her bulldog teeth. She straightened her back and charged in for the final push.

A balding man with black hair joined me and sat back to witness the exchange.

I knew Lola had lost long before the words left her mouth. My mathematical husband would never have been convinced that the cost was worth it. $22,500 for a studio unit, alternating weeks in a bi-annual contract, $500 maintenance fee extra. *Not a chance.*

John tried to demonstrate in logical language the multiple ways this didn't make sense. But Lola continued on as if Fermat himself had possessed her with his greatest enigma. I was sitting there, imagining us coming to Hawaii for the rest of our lives. The three-panel color brochure of the condo timeshare complex glowed in my hands. The phrase "We'll leave the porch light on for you every year" glistened on the bottom of the back fold. I was certain this timeshare was meant to be.

All of the sudden, my fantasy was interrupted. Lola stood up. She whipped her straight-edged hair sideways and announced: "This feels like a waste of my time. Why you'd want to waste my time and our company's time is beyond me." In a flash, she was gone. The platter of small cinnamon rolls was whisked away. The balding man put his head down and rocked it side to side as if we were great disappointments to him.

"Can we think about this overnight?" I asked.

He raised his eyes. "Well, for you? We will offer you twenty-four hours. But don't tell anyone. They'll think I'm going soft."

"Could we get more cinnamon rolls?" I asked. Did I say it because I needed to do whatever it took to soften the moment? The reality of having these people not like me was so uncomfortable.

I never did get the extra cinnamon rolls.

John awakened me from my dream by standing up and walking boldly away from the table.

I called out to him, "Hey John! Wait a second. We need to book some excursions. We get discounts now."

"I don't care anymore," John said. "These people are crooks."

How dare he call these two lovely people who were simply trying to sell us a vacation in Hawaii crooks? (Yes, I know what you're thinking—Did Brian just fall off a pineapple truck on Lanai? Let's just say my wisdom about finances and investment is not my most endearing quality.) Next to a small table near the exit stood the excursion manager, Ken, a white guy with a prototypical Hawaiian shirt and safari hat (you never know when you'll need a safari hat in Hawaii). We learned later that Ken was from Idaho. He was grinning excitedly.

After letting Ken know that we did not purchase a timeshare contract, he said, "Well, not everyone is wise enough to take advantage of a special deal like this. But don't let that get you down. You've got some adventures to have! Remember, this discount is only good for the next seven days."

John already had his hand on the exit door. I stood there, hoping Ken would give us the keys to the kingdom so we could experience the real Hawaii. Then, a swishy, stunning queen in his sixties named Tian, "authentically from Hawaii" (as he reminded me many times in our dialogue), came from behind the information desk and placed his arm over my shoulder. "Ken, I've got these boys," he said. "They're family."

Being gay at times is kinda like having a Platinum American Express card, because at times we notice one another and open doors for one another in lovely ways. After repeating that his lineage was the northern part of the island of Hawaii, he pulled my grouchy husband and me over to what I will forever call "the secret super gay special activity desk" and sat us down. If you're gay, you've likely had this happen to you. Remember this is twenty years ago, so the term "gay marriage" was not even on our lips.

"Okay, boys!" Tian announced. "I know what you're doing. Please skip the lame booze cruises where straight people will be drunk, vomiting to the song 'American Pie.' That pie doesn't have a slice for you. Am I right, ladies?"

John looked exasperated and tired. He started to stand up. Tian looked at John. "Not all of us can be queens, can we darling?" He looked at me.

I replied, "Some of us are more "Mary" than others. I'm definitely the more "Mary" of this team." Gay humor has always eluded me, but I thought that was a pretty good response. I remember it to this day, because I thought the gay supreme council would have approved.

Tian said, "All right, what does Mr. John and Mrs. Mary like to do?"

"Hiking!" I yelled. I couldn't wait to get the process moving.

Tian replied, "Well honey, you don't need a discount to get dirty and climb a hill. Get out there and get dirty! That's how I like my men anyway. Do you know what I mean, Mary?"

I nodded but my timing was clearly delayed. The uncomfortable gay joke died. I loved Tian, I love all gay men who claim their space in the world and require people to take notice. He was my fearless leader...I was certain that Pelé had been reborn in Tian's lovely, sun-parched body (which was, in my opinion, begging for lotion). John looked at his watch multiple times. The nightmare of the timeshare experience was waiting to end outside that door, but I was blocking the exit.

Tian continued. "Well, I can see you are in a rush, Mr. John. I'll suggest one ultimate excursion. It is sure to provide you with a lot of walking unless you get an ass to carry you. No, honey, that's not a gay joke. Although, it surely should be. There are real asses to carry you down the trail."
I said, "Is it on this island?"
"Be patient, Mary. I'm getting there. Let me relish my ass joke." Then, a serious expression emerged. Tian leaned in. "I strongly recommend you do the Damien Tours Excursion on the lush, secluded island of Molokai. You will visit a national park very few Americans even know exist. You will forever thank me if you say "Yes!" to this excursion."

John bent forward. "Tian, thank you for your time, but we are not flying to Molokai."

Tian raised his hand, and pretended to be touching a magical calculator. "I can include your roundtrip airfare and excursion for $150 per person, normally over $350 per person. You must do this excursion. I'll make an agreement with you, Mr. John. If you are in any way unpleased with the trip, I will pay for it when you return."

The air around our small, special, gay, secret-deal table stilled. I knew we were headed for the adventure of a lifetime. I pictured us gliding across Hawaiian rainforests, suspended from roots hanging from a large canopy of trees. I envisioned us finding the perfect Blue Hawaiian on the perfect beach. We paid with Visa. I'm pretty sure John thought the card would explode at any moment.

Mrs. Mary and Mr. John walked out of that timeshare meeting beleaguered and exhausted. John was more hurt than I realized, but our walk across the small cliff separating Big Beach from Little Beach allowed him to reconnect with the beauty of the island.

* * *

At 6:00 a.m., the plane engines roared, three other people boarded the eight-seater plane and the young female pilot (from South Carolina) stepped into the cockpit. The plane went up and then immediately started to descend. I felt as if I could touch the tops of mountains with my toes. John looked incredulous and joyful, and the blue ocean and stunning scenery had him taking photo after photo of the world beneath us.

As we touched down on the runway, the pilot announced, "Molokai is my favorite island. This jewel of the Hawaiian archipelago will likely call your name again. Welcome to Molokai!" She said every word with great joy. I felt as though she was speaking directly to me.

After getting our rental car and directions, we headed to the trailhead for our excursion. Our job was to descend the trail from the top of the cliff to an isolated location. At the bottom of the trail, our tour guide was to meet us.

"We need to get going, so we get ahead of the asses," said John.

"Can we not call them that? That just sounds weird," I said.

"That's what they are," John said. "I don't want a bunch of asses pooping in front of us on the trail. That will be disgusting." Then, we both smiled.

The signs on the trail state clearly that visitors are not allowed to descend the trail without being accompanied by a set tour. I felt the two folded-up sheets of paper in my shorts pocket—*our tour passes*?—I had them.

"Are you seriously not seeing this sign, John? Really?"

John grabbed the fanny pack with matching water bottles hastily and secured it around his waist, on top of his grey rain jacket. Never sexier. He began to descend the trail. As we zig-zagged down the cliff-side trail, the vistas were dramatic. One can only imagine who built this original trail. We left a part of ourselves at the top of that trail. The beauty was overwhelming, I knew we would never fully reclaim who we had been before we started down the side of that cliff.

I don't think any person making this pilgrimage could ever be the same. As Kapalua National Park comes into view, you can see that this stretch of land is completely isolated. The rough, intense ocean waves that are home to hammerhead and tiger sharks would make any water escape impossible, and the sharp cliffs would be impossible to traverse without ropes. In our summary materials, it states that the authorities would shoot people who tried to escape using the cliff trail. The story we would soon learn about this location was incredible.

As we hit the valley below, the silence was deafening. The songs of birds and ocean waves win here. We walked the quarter mile to meet the tour, and the adventurers who chose to ride the mules down the cliff eventually caught up with us. The large, pointed ears of these peaceful creatures began to soften as the Hawaiian print shirt-clad tourists climbed off of them, camera bags swinging. They scurried about, spreading sunscreen on each other and making jokes about how they wished our hosts served Corona beer on the tour.

Our group of twelve stood, our white tour passes blowing in the wind, waiting for the tour bus. All of a sudden, a yellow school bus approached. A lovely man with a wild beard stepped off the bus. He smiled from ear-to-ear as he greeted each of us. We climbed onto the bus. He never asked for our sheets of paper. He just started to tell his story of how he arrived at this place in the middle of the Hawaiian archipelago.

Kapalua was the place where, starting in the 1860's, the authorities exiled many native Hawaiians with Hansen's Disease—the disease also known as Leprosy. Bounty hunters were paid a fee for rounding up infected people, who were then forced onto boats to be resettled in this colony below the cliffs. The settlement is still active and cares for residents who have been there for many years. At its height, there were over one thousand residents. Well over 8,000 people called this place home and completed their lives here.

"I'm Martin," the bus driver told us. "I was a young boy when I was brought here, and I was separated from my parents at the time. I never saw them again, but this became my new home and my new family." I watched and listened as this charming man steered the big bus around the curves of the dirt road leading into the small town. Every word punched me in the gut. He had told his story so many times to so many people...I loved him immediately. Back home, the AIDS epidemic was destroying families, taking many lives as our nation struggled with how to respond to a disease that was killing mostly gay men at the time. The symmetry was not lost on me. Ryan White had already died, and the names of many men had been sewn into quilts honoring each one—the same quilts a crowd of half a million people visited on the mall in D.C. in 1987.

A woman directly behind me called out to Martin, saying, "I'm sorry to interrupt, but I don't understand why my twelve-year-old and my eight-year-old couldn't come on this tour. They need to hear this story. Is it the mule ride or the cliff environment that creates the age requirement?"

Martin pulled over and turned his brown eyes to us. He responded in a somber voice, "We have the age requirement of sixteen, because we must honor that many of our residents had their children ripped from their arms when they were forced into exile here. We protect that pain. Only the memories of our own children can fill our streets, or the hearts of our people would break every day when your children left. That loss would occur every day and remind them of the children they never saw again."

The bus grew silent, and Martin continued with his guided history tour as he drove us up and down the streets of the little town, showing us the medical clinic, the pharmacy still in operation, and the cemetery. At the end of our tour, Martin took us to the Catholic Church on the island. It featured many pictures honoring Saint Damien, the Catholic priest who contracted Hansen's disease when he was serving here. He died in Kapalua, and he helped to unite the community. As Martin stood outside the church, the Catholic parish priest showed us around and told us the story of Father Damien. He ended by telling us about our driver and tour guide, Martin, with whom we had spent the last four hours.

"Martin is not just the tour guide for Damien Tours," he told us. "He serves every member of this community tirelessly, even though he is sixty-nine years old. When you leave, he will drive that school bus up and down the streets of our little village and check on people until late in the evening. If a person has their porch light on, he will go and spend some time with them. He provides emotional support, gets them medications, and prays with people. He never takes a day off, and he is the most joyful man I've ever met."

On our drive from the church back to the grassy patch where our tour started, I watched Martin closely. He smiled his broad smile as the bus crossed the dips and potholes on the broken-down dirt road, and his stories filled the bus. He had cast a spell on me, and I knew that I had met a real hero. Martin taught me that when you see every challenging experience in life as a call to action for others, you will always have a purpose in this life.

A man ripped from the arms of his mother and exiled to this bizarre thumb of land jutting off the island of Molokai found joy in pain, a purpose in suffering, and he lit a light in the heart of every soul he met.

His smile was earned, and it proved that a purpose is where heartfelt joy occurs.

ACKNOWLEDGEMENTS

I wanted to take a moment to thank any person who assisted me in writing this book. The love and support I have been offered throughout this process has been another example to me of Spirit's gift in my life. I know I will forget some names, and I hope you will forgive me if that occurred here.

I had many editors, first readers, and friends who, along the way, believed in the intentions that guided this book and showed up in powerful ways for me.

Thank you, Mikey for teaching me that I, too, could be a writer. Thank you to Colleen, Holly, Janice, Love, Margaret, Constance, Kim, Alaine, Deb Kiva (the best astrologer in the world), and John for reading this book in multiple forms along the way and guiding me to create the best book possible. Thank you, John Paul for your vision and your brilliance in guiding my creative process. You are a true gem. Thanks Marcia for listening to this idea on a porch in the summer where you fought off an anaconda for me.

Thank you to my mentor, Jenn, for always asking the hard questions and for being a reincarnation of Yoda. I must also thank the Bolts of Love Leadership Team, especially Kim Griffin for always seeing the hope and loving the same television show with zombies and hot men. I also need to thank Cheri for being a healer to all people and to Stacey for keeping it real.

I am also so touched and humbled that Colin Bates, a person I have never met in life, agreed to read my text and also write the foreword. That speaks to his humility and sincere love of all who are called to this work.

Thank you, John for believing in me as a medium far sooner than I believed in myself. He proves that love changes us and moves us in directions we never could have traveled without that support. John's family has become my family over the years, and this sense of belonging and love has provided me the security to take the risk to offer this book to the world.

Finally, thanks mom for everything. I always knew you were my Thelma, but I never knew I was your Louise.

ABOUT THE AUTHOR

Brian E. Bowles works as an evidential medium and he spends most of his time in Ferndale, Washington. Brian has received master's degrees in the fields of Education and Counseling Psychology with an emphasis in family therapy prior to honoring his calling in mediumship.

Because of Brian's health circumstances, he only offers limited readings per month.

If you are interested in reaching out to connect with him, please check out his website where you can schedule your time with him there.

www.halfwaythroughthewoods.com

Made in the USA
Monee, IL
21 March 2020